30 HERITAGE BUILDINGS OF YANGON

First published in 2012 by Association of Myanmar Architects
in association with Serindia Publications, Inc.

Research & Text: Sarah Rooney
Contributions: Su Lin Lewis, Dagon Taya, U Thaw Kaung
Editorial Management: Lyndal Barry, Sue Mark, Daw Moe Moe Lwin
Book Design: Natthaphat Meksriwan
Publisher: Shane Suvikapakornkul (Serindia Publications)

10 9 8 7 6 5 4 3 2

Second printing with corrections: October 2013

ISBN 978-1-932476-62-0 (Hardcover)

Library of Congress Cataloging-in-Publication Data

Rooney, Sarah
30 heritage buildings of Yangon / text by Sarah Rooney.
p. cm.
"[Published in association with] Association of Myanmar Architects."
Includes bibliographical references and index.
Summary: "This volume is a compilation of 30 important colonial-era buildings in Yangon, Myanmar. It provides the history of each building and is illustrated with both present and old photographs"--Provided by publisher.
ISBN 978-1-932476-62-0 (hardcover : alk. paper) -- ISBN 978-1-932476-63-7 (softcover : alk. paper)
1. Architecture--Burma--Rangoon--History. 2. Architecture--Conservation and restoration--Burma--Rangoon. 3. Rangoon (Burma)--Buildings, structures, etc. I. Association of Myanmar Architects. II. Title. III. Title: Thirty heritage buildings of Yangon.
NA1512.2.R36R66 2012
720.9591--dc23

2012013190

30 HERITAGE BUILDINGS OF YANGON

INSIDE THE CITY THAT CAPTURED TIME

ASSOCIATION OF MYANMAR ARCHITECTS

Association of
Myanmar Architects

Serindia Publications, Chicago

TABLE OF CONTENTS

FOREWORD

Rangoon, or Yangon as she is now again known under her Myanmar name, is my hometown: the place where I was born and where I grew up, where I was educated and lived through war and peace with frequent turmoil, and where I hope to pass the rest of my life. I have a warm attachment to this city, capital of Myanmar, which is a place of greenery enriched by huge trees, colourful flowers, placid lakes, parks, pagodas and monasteries; a place I have enjoyed living in for the last seven decades and more.

Yangon is steeped in history. As a Mon village, she was known first as Dagon after the golden Shwedagon Pagoda in whose shadow she grew for over a thousand years. Then, in May 1755, King Alaungpaya renamed her Yangon ("the end of strife") after he had conquered and finally crushed the ancient Mon Kingdom.

Although I have lived abroad on several occasions for about two or three years at a time – mainly in and around London, UK – I have always longed to return to Yangon for her peace and quiet, friendly people, and the lovely colonial buildings where I have been able to live and work.

I think I am very fortunate to have had the opportunity to live in some of the large colonial style houses, built from the start of the 20th century to about the end of the 1920s. When I was born in 1937, my father, U Kaung, was Headmaster of the Rangoon Government High School and we lived in a black-timbered building built on high stilt-like teak posts right opposite the grand Victorian splendour of the sprawling Rangoon General Hospital on Commissioner (now Bogyoke Aung San) Road. Later, as my father moved up in the official education sector to become the first Burmese Buddhist Director of Education after Independence, our family was able to reside in some of the best colonial government residences in Windermere Court, and later Windermere Crescent a few doors away from Prime Minister U Nu's residence. U Thant, who later became the UN Secretary-General, lived on the lane behind our house, just a few doors away, while he was working as the Prime Minister's Secretary. His government residence, another large colonial building painted the usual light yellow and set in a spacious garden, was right at the southern edge of Windermere Park, which being on a ridge (the British preferred high ground for their official residences), had a superb view of the Shwedagon Pagoda. U Thant, who was five years younger than my father, was his close friend because both had worked as headmasters before World War II. Fortunately, all these residential buildings built around 1923 in the area called Windermere Park remain today and are still used as official residences of the present Greater Yangon Region high government officials.

From 1970 to 1997 when I retired as Chief Librarian of the Universities Central Library, I lived with my family in a big colonial house on the Yangon University main campus. The house had cool verandas all around it and was situated on about one acre of garden land where we grew mangoes, durians, jackfruits, and many flowering trees and plants.

My place of work from 1959, when I first graduated, was the white two-storied Rangoon University Library building whose foundation stone was laid on 8 December 1927, a gift from a wealthy Indian merchant Raja S. Ramanathan Reddiar and his two wives [the donor carefully inscribed that one wife was deceased!]. When it was built in the late 1920s it was noted as one of the best library buildings in the whole of Southeast Asia.

The government and commercial buildings I used to visit were also mainly built during the late 19th and early 20th centuries. I remember the many visits I had to make to the offices of the ministers and government ministries, which used to be located in the old British Secretariat building. I also had to go to the Customs House to clear all electrical appliances and even used household items brought back from sojourns overseas. And I went often to the grand Jubilee Hall and the hybrid Myanmar-Western-style City Hall, which at different times after Independence used to house the Myanmar National Library. Unfortunately, Jubilee Hall, which was lavishly decorated with exquisite Myanmar carvings, was demolished [unnecessarily] in the early 1990s to make way for a rather nondescript modern museum.

For shopping, my wife and I used to visit Rowe & Company right next to City Hall; it was for many decades the best department store in our country. And I remember well the many wedding receptions we attended at the Strand Hotel, one of the oldest and best hotels in town, and also at the Chin Tsong Palace, which after Independence was leased by the Strand Hotel for a number of years.

It was only in the last decade of the 20th century that modern hotels and residences, shopping malls, flats and condos, and new government and private office buildings began to appear all over Yangon with the "opening up" of the country. An author on Myanmar has written that the term "opened up" is an unpleasantly "eviscerative phrase", like a painful but unavoidable surgical operation. Modernization brings painful side effects. For me the loss of some of the most aesthetically pleasing colonial buildings is one of the worst consequences of this rapid globalization process. But it is, I think, a side effect that can be avoided if we are aware of their value, their history, and the benefits that the conservation and preservation of these beautiful old buildings can bring to our country and our people.

This new book, beautifully written with pleasing photographs, is to be commended for raising awareness, not only in Myanmar but in other countries also, of the beauty, value, and importance of some of the very best colonial buildings of Yangon so that efforts can be made to preserve them; once these buildings are gone, an important part of our life, history, and heritage will be lost forever.

Thaw Kaung
Part-time Member, Myanmar Historical Commission
Retired Chief Librarian, Universities Central Library

HITACHI

INTRODUCTION

"Architecture is all too often imagined as if buildings do not – and should not – change. But they do, and have always done. Buildings are gifts, and because they are, we must pass them on."

— Edward Hollis, *The Secret Lives of Buildings*

The modern history of Yangon can be traced through its colonial-era buildings and the imprint of the past is indelibly marked on the life cycle of each remaining structure. The stories of these buildings are intimately entwined with the people who built them, the memories of those who lived and worked within them, and the reality of those who live and work there still. The Myawaddy Bank [9] building on Sule Pagoda Road, for instance, was once the Reserve Bank of India and the central financial arm of the British Empire; each critical development in the history of Myanmar's currency has been channelled through its walls from the introduction of overprinted Indian rupee notes to the first Burmese *kyat* and the demonitisations of the socialist era. Certainly no building better symbolises Yangon's cosmopolitan past than the former Sofaer's Buildings [13] on Pansodan Street. Built by a Baghdadi Jewish trader in the early 1900s, Sofaer's housed an Egyptian cigar shop, the photographic studio of a famous German photographer, the head office of Reuters news agency in Myanmar, and a hair salon run by a former circus performer from the Philippines. These are just a few of the names and trades from around the globe that settled in Sofaer's Buildings at one time or another, and vestiges of these cosmopolitan inhabitants still cling to its now dilapidated form.

The many colonial-era buildings that survive in Yangon have, inevitably, weathered over the years. Some state their origins proudly with brass wall plaques or marble foundation stones. Others retain only fleeting hints of their former occupants – a set of initials inscribed on a wall or the shadow of a name beneath peeling layers of paint. In some cases, their structures have been altered and adjusted to suit the changing needs of their occupants; interiors have been partitioned, windows bricked over, air-conditioning vents knocked through, and alternative entrances opened up.

A number of buildings are still being used for their original purpose. St. Paul's [3] has been a high school since it was built in 1885. The Strand Hotel [20], constructed over a century ago, is still accommodating visitors to the city. Many of the buildings have been repurposed. What was once the headquarters of a pioneering 19th-century Scottish trading firm is now an embassy, an ostentatious private mansion has become an art school, and a former department store later used as a government ministry currently stands empty. Whatever their condition and use, these buildings represent a unique and valuable legacy. The sheer density of surviving colonial-era buildings – from rows of humble shop houses to grand edifices of Empire – is unparalleled within the Southeast Asian region.

Ian Morley, an urban historian at the Chinese University of Hong Kong, has described these buildings as "the last example of a 'colonial core' still intact in Asia". As Morley puts it, "Yangon presents itself as a city that time forgot, but I'd say it's a city that captured time."

The physical setting within which Yangon's colonial-era buildings are set first began to take shape in simple sketches drawn by a British superintendent surgeon called Dr William Montgomerie over 150 years ago. Montgomerie had arrived in Yangon with British troops in 1852 and brought with him some town planning experience as a member of the Singapore town committee when Sir Stamford Raffles mapped out the new city of Singapore. Impressed by the commercially advantageous riverside setting, Montgomerie proposed a wide Strand along the river that would be kept clear of buildings and plotted a grid of streets leading off it at right angles. Such a design would help keep the city cool as the streets would channel the river breeze and rows of buildings would provide shade for the opposite side of each street, except at midday.

Shortly after those early drawings were submitted, the job of planning Yangon was officially tasked to Lieutenant Alexander Fraser, of the Bengal Engineers. Fraser expanded Montgomerie's chessboard pattern and placed the Sule Pagoda just east of centre on the grid. At that time, the northern reaches of the city-to-be, located around the Shwedagon Pagoda, were being used as a military cantonment and so were excluded from these early plans – a division that can still be felt today as Yangon exists in two distinct parts with the downtown area presenting a dense, geometrically precise layout while the areas beyond it are mapped out on a rambling and expansive network of winding lanes and roundabouts.

B. R. Pearn, who authored the comprehensive study *A History of Rangoon* (1939), was not overly enamoured by this plan. He wrote that it was unoriginal as the grid was an obvious pattern used by Valentine Knight to rebuild London after the Great Fire of 1666 and the streets were too narrow for health and cleanliness in a tropical city. He also noted that, in the British zeal to create the new capital, almost all vestiges of the Burmese settlements that preceded it were obliterated, with the exception of the monasteries and pagodas.

Montgomerie was right about Yangon's commercial potential and the town rapidly outgrew Fraser's original design, which had anticipated a city of 36,000 inhabitants. Within less than a decade the population had nearly doubled to

60,000. By the beginning of the 20th century the population was increasing by 5,000 a year as the economy flourished, driven by the so-called "trinity" of industries on which the city's wealth was built – paddy, oil, and teak.

The logistical challenges of turning the swampy riverside location into a modern metropolis were enormous. The entire town had to be raised by two-to-three feet – a process that involved the transportation of vast amounts of earth from north of the city [in just one year, during the 1860s, four million cubic feet of earth was deposited in what is today the downtown area]. By the time Fraser's plan had been fully implemented around 1870, the area to the west of Godwin [today, Lanmadaw] Street had already expanded with the addition of four new roads on the grid. On the other side, east of Sparks [now Bo Aung Kyaw] Street was still a marshy wilderness of paddy fields and the occasional timber yard. With the ever-increasing population and a limited municipal budget, the city authorities struggled to provide adequate sewage and water systems and it was not until the late 1880s that proper systems were introduced; even then, their coverage was far from comprehensive and the city was generally considered, in the words of B. R. Pearn, "a thoroughly unhealthy place to live in".

The early decades of the 20th century saw a construction boom as the colonial administration upgraded and expanded its earlier offices, merchant houses established their headquarters, international banks opened new branches, and smaller shops grew into large department stores and bazaars. In keeping with the British town-planning concept of a "garden city", open green spaces were created and maintained such as the Royal [Kandawgyi] Lake, zoological gardens, and cantonment park around the Shwedagon pagoda. As the city continued to spread northwards, the government Public Works Department found itself yet again filling in hitherto uninhabitable swampland. In 1925, the chairman of the city's Development Trust illustrated just how much the city had grown when he explained that the Sule Pagoda, located in the downtown grid near the river, had once been at the city's centre; by the time the Trust had finished its land reclamation projects, the Shwedagon pagoda, which is situated much further inland, had become the new geographical heart of the city.

In 1945, the US serviceman and author John L. Christian described a thoroughly modern city in his book *Burma*: "Rangoon was a city of electric lights, paved streets, cinemas, night spots, garish neon signs and all the comforts of home... Some of its buildings, such as the Port [Authority building], the Irrawaddy Flotilla Company's headquarters, the Imperial Bank of India, the National Bank of India, were as modern as any to be found in an American or European city of the same size."

Yangon's colonial-era buildings are survivors. They have lived through war and natural disasters, as well as numerous changes of ownership and systems of government. They withstood the bombs of World War II that were dropped on the city first by the invading Japanese army and later by Allied forces reclaiming the city in 1945. The Yangon Division Court [22] stands as an evocative testimony to this period; its northern wing was destroyed during the war and never repaired. Most recently, in 2008, the buildings survived the devastating winds of Cyclone Nargis, which tore down trees and stripped off much of the city's roofing.

Today, the biggest threat to these buildings is neglect. When the government shifted the capital of Myanmar to Nay Pyi Taw at the end of 2005, it left behind a huge array of state-owned buildings that were once occupied by ministries and government departments. Many of these now stand empty, are only partially occupied, or will be shifted in the near future. Without daily occupancy and regular maintenance, the buildings are falling prey to damp, rust, weeds, and termites – all of which will accelerate their eventual decay. Architects estimate that, without immediate attention, the buildings now have a limited lifespan of between 10-to-30 years.

Currently, the legal framework for protecting these buildings comes under the remit of the city's municipal body, the Yangon City Development Committee [YCDC], which has a heritage list of 189 public buildings in Yangon that were constructed before 1930 and have a distinctive architectural style. Potential developers must seek permission from the YCDC to alter or demolish a listed building. After the government's move to Nay Pyi Taw, the disused public buildings came under the jurisdiction and care of the Ministry of Construction's Department of Human Settlements and Housing Development.

In regards to heritage preservation, Daw Hlaing Maw Oo, Assistant Director of the Department of Human Settlement and Housing Development, favours a holistic approach that focuses not just on individual structures but on the ecology of the city as a whole. "I am concerned with both the tangible and intangible heritage of our city, which means the buildings themselves as well as the lives that are lived in and around them," she says. "In Yangon we still have a lot of this 'living' heritage as we have atmosphere and social networks that have built up around, and grown within, these old buildings over many decades. It would be very interesting indeed if we could preserve these as well. To do this, we need to establish a conceptual framework so that we can understand how the past – as embodied in these buildings – can provide us with an effective link to the future."

As a link between the past and the future, the options for Yangon's colonial-era buildings are plentiful. With a rising middle class in Yangon and the growth of international tourism there will be an increased demand for access to leisure activities and tourism services in the city. These buildings can potentially serve as offices, hotels, institutions, museums, restaurants, bars, shopping complexes, department stores, residential units, art galleries, and theatres or cinemas. For the larger buildings, there is also the possibility of mixed-use space with, for example, a collection of art galleries being combined with artists' studios or an art school. Identifying financially sustainable uses will enable long-term investment and maintenance. Past experience within the region has taught that partnerships are key to this process, especially those between government entities and the private sector. Successful plans tend to incorporate and galvanise all sectors of society, from the municipal authorities and urban middle class to small business enterprises and youth.

Indeed, local architects and urban planners involved in heritage preservation point to the need for authentic reinterpretations of old buildings that will take into account the existing social fabric. Proper choices in their repurposing can boost the buildings' economic potential to create new jobs and improve the surrounding urban environment. In short, Yangon is at a critical crossroads – the city that captured time now has an opportunity to enhance its legacy and offer a new lease of life to its historic buildings and the communities around them.

This book examines some 30 buildings in Yangon that were selected by members of the Association of Myanmar Architects [AMA] for their architectural and historical significance. They range in age from the now derelict Pegu Club [28], built in 1882, to the art deco Chartered Bank [17] building completed in 1941 just a year before the Japanese invasion in World War II. The list is by no means comprehensive and focuses primarily on public buildings; for reasons of space and practicality, religious structures and private residences have not been included.

Piecing together the social history of a building involves delving into out-of-print books, company records, old city directories, newspaper archives, and people's memories. As stories are compiled from a wide variety sources, in both English and Burmese languages, old and new links between buildings and people have emerged. The aim of this book is simply to contribute to the collective conversation about the social and economic potential of Yangon's colonial-era heritage in the hopes that the city's diverse past can become a vibrant and sustainable part of its future.

MAP : 30 HERITAGE BUILDINGS OF YANGON

List of buildings: overleaf

PAZUNDAUNG CREEK
BOGYOKE AUNG SAN ROAD
ANAWRAHTA ROAD
MAHABANDOOLA ROAD
MERCHANT ROAD
STRAND ROAD
MAHABANDOOLA GARDEN STREET
PANSODAN STREET
SEIKANTHAR STREET
BO AUNG KYAW STREET
THEINBYU ROAD
1
2
3
5
7
8
11
12
13
14
15
16
17
18
19
20
21
22
23

A. AROUND THE SECRETARIAT

1. MINISTERS' OFFICE
   [Secretariat]
2. PRINTING & PUBLISHING ENTERPRISE
   [Government Press]
3. B.E. HIGH SCHOOL 6 BOTAHTAUNG
   [St. Paul's High School]

B. AROUND SULE PAGODA

4. CITY HALL
5. IMMIGRATION DEPARTMENT
   [Rowe & Co. Department Store]
6. FORMER MINISTRY OF HOTELS & TOURISM
7. CENTRAL TELEGRAPH OFFICE
8. HIGH COURT

C. MERCHANT ROAD, THE BANKING QUARTERS

9. MYAWADDY BANK
   [Reserve Bank of India]
10. MYANMAR OIL & GAS ENTERPRISE
    [Burmah Oil Company]
11. MERCHANT ROAD BANKS

D. PANSODAN STREET, LOWER BLOCK

12. INTERNAL REVENUE DEPARTMENT
    [Rander House]
13. LOKANAT GALLERY BUILDING
    [Sofaer's Buildings]
14. INLAND WATERWAYS DEPARTMENT
    [Irrawaddy Flotilla Company]
15. MYANMAR AGRICULTURAL DEVELOPMENT BANK
    [Grindlays Bank]
16. MYANMAR ECONOMIC BANK 1
    [Lloyds Bank]
17. MYANMAR ECONOMIC BANK 2
    [Chartered Bank]

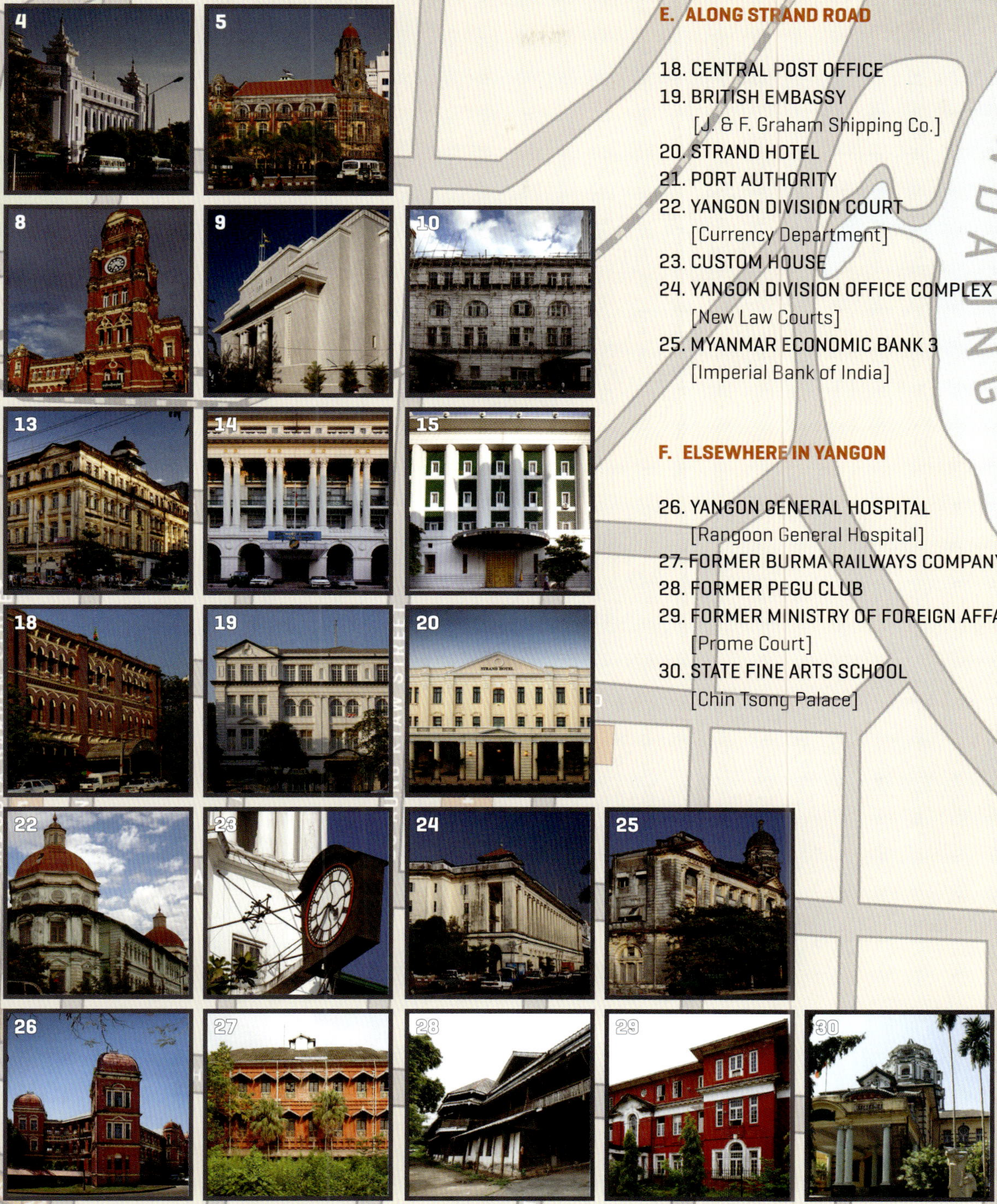

E. ALONG STRAND ROAD

18. CENTRAL POST OFFICE
19. BRITISH EMBASSY
    [J. & F. Graham Shipping Co.]
20. STRAND HOTEL
21. PORT AUTHORITY
22. YANGON DIVISION COURT
    [Currency Department]
23. CUSTOM HOUSE
24. YANGON DIVISION OFFICE COMPLEX
    [New Law Courts]
25. MYANMAR ECONOMIC BANK 3
    [Imperial Bank of India]

F. ELSEWHERE IN YANGON

26. YANGON GENERAL HOSPITAL
    [Rangoon General Hospital]
27. FORMER BURMA RAILWAYS COMPANY
28. FORMER PEGU CLUB
29. FORMER MINISTRY OF FOREIGN AFFAIRS
    [Prome Court]
30. STATE FINE ARTS SCHOOL
    [Chin Tsong Palace]

A AROUND THE SECRETARIAT

This area was once the seat of power of the British colonial government. Dominated by the overwhelming presence of the former Secretariat buildings, which became the **Ministers' Office (1)** after Independence, it is now a quiet and relatively unpopulated neighbourhood as the old Secretariat stands mostly empty. Across the road to the north is **Basic Education High School 6 Botahtaung (3)**, originally St. Paul's High School run by Catholic missionary brothers. On Theinbyu Road to the east is the **Printing & Publishing Enterprise (2)**, formerly the Government Press during British times.

The southern and western sides of the Secretariat compound are also lined with colonial-era structures. Along Mahabandoola Road to the south are the Haroon Soorty, or "Harsoorty" Mansions, built in 1928-1929 by Indian textile traders and the Ibrahim Buildings constructed around the same time – both are fine examples of shop house architecture with the ground floor being used for commercial purposes and the upper floors for residences. Today, this stretch of road is crowded with small business enterprises that include street vendors, teashops, photocopy shops, and general goods stores. Strolling beneath the covered walkway in front of the Harsoorty Mansions, it is easy to catch a glimpse of what bustling 1930s Rangoon must have been like.

When the 1930 earthquake struck the city, it was buildings built on soft, alluvial soil that suffered the most, such as the Secretariat which lost its turrets and central dome. This rare photograph of its southern wing shows them still intact before the earthquake.

SEA GREEN

1 MINISTERS' OFFICE

formerly
SECRETARIAT

Location:
300 Theinbyu Road, between Anawrahta Road and Mahabandoola Road

Built: 1889-1905

Architect/ Contractor:
Henry Hoyne-Fox (architect), Baboo Naitram Rambux (contractor)

Judged on scale and grandeur, the former Secretariat is the most spectacular colonial-era building in Yangon. Designed as the administrative seat of the colonial government, this sprawling Victorian structure was disparagingly referred to by British residents as "bureaucratic Byzantine" in style.

PAST

After the British annexation of Upper Burma in 1886, the colonial government's administrative work increased exponentially and there was an urgent need to expand the cramped and poorly lit Secretariat, which was originally located on Strand Road. Designs for grand new premises were drawn by Henry Hoyne-Fox, Executive Engineer at the government's Public Works Department in Yangon. Hoyne-Fox designed numerous important government buildings in the city including Rangoon General Hospital (26), the original law courts (24), and the President's House, the last two of which have since been demolished. He was an architect of the old school who exported the grandiloquent Victorian aesthetic to the East.

The new Secretariat was constructed in stages. Construction on the southern wing, which runs along Mahabandoola (then Dalhousie) Road, began in 1889 and was fraught with difficulty. Builders were hampered by soggy ground in the plot's west corner, where there had once been a water tank, and this was further complicated by a particularly torrential monsoon season. Water had to be continuously bailed out of the building site. To stabilise the soil, *pyinkado* logs (an extremely hard timber grown in Myanmar) that were 13-20 feet long had to be driven into the soil and topped with a grid of iron rails. The southern axis was finally completed in 1893 and, to this day, rumours persist that it is sinking into the swamp below.

In 1903, construction began on the additional east and west wings, which were duly completed by 1905. The contractor was careful not to repeat previous mistakes. During construction of the south wing, work had been brought to a standstill when artificial stone ordered for the decorative details failed to arrive; to prevent similar delays in consecutive wings, stone was manufactured on site.

Once completed, the entire colony was effectively run from the Secretariat. The departments housed within its labyrinthine halls, the number of which is a testament to the fastidious organizational might of the British Empire, included the following departments: Political, General, Police, Revenue, Forest, Financial (Accounts, Separate Revenue, Local Funds), Judicial (Arms,

Criminal, Civil, Jails, Lunatics, Legislature, Penal Settlements], Municipal [Books & Maps, Education, Ecclesiastical, Registration, Medical, Sanitary], and Marine and Commerce [Lighthouses, Ports, Merchant Shipping]. Each of these departments was staffed by a veritable army of secretaries, clerks, stenographers, statisticians, and record-keepers.

The building was not overly popular with those who worked there and was described in a memoir written by E. C. V. Foucar, a British barrister and member of the Legislative Council during the 1930s, as an "ugly, vast and insanitary building". After working hours, however, its demeanour was transformed; the hundreds of government clerks filed off home and the gardens were opened to the general public who came to enjoy the cool of the early evening, picnicking and playing *chinlon* [a Burmese ball game played with a rattan ball].

Each critical step towards the country's independence from British rule was marked within this compound: The establishment of diarchy in 1923, the Burma Legislative Council elections on separation from India in 1932, and the evolution of the Government of Burma Act 1935 which was put into force when Burma separated from India in 1937 and led to Dr. Ba Maw becoming the first Burmese Prime Minister.

On 20 December 1938, student demonstrators protesting against British rule surrounded the building to press for the release of fellow activists imprisoned by the authorities. Mounted police dispersed the crowd and a student called Aung Kyaw was killed after being hit on the head with a police truncheon. The street that runs along the west side of the Secretariat compound is now called Bo Aung Kyaw Street in his memory.

The single most significant event to take place inside the Secretariat building happened on the morning of 19 July 1947, just six months before Myanmar's independence from Britain. On that day, national leader and founder of the Burmese army General Aung San and six ministerial colleagues were assassinated while attending a meeting of the Executive Council in the southwest corner of the building. It was an event that changed the course of Burmese history. Today, the room in which they were assassinated is maintained as a shrine; those who died there became known as martyrs. Martyrs' Day [*Azani Ney*] is still commemorated annually with activities that focus around the Martyrs' Mausoleum near the Shwedagon Pagoda.

Myanmar's independence was duly marked inside the quadrangle of the Secretariat compound at 4.20 a.m. on 4 January 1948. It was here that the Union Jack was solemnly lowered for the final time to the tune of *God Save*

General Aung San, the charismatic leader of Myanmar's struggle for independence from the British and founding father of the Burmese army, was killed in the Secretariat building on 19 July 1947.

the King and the flag of the Union of Burma was raised as a band played the Burmese national anthem, *Kaba Ma Kyei* [Till the End of the World]. U Ba U, who was Chief Justice of Yangon at the time and would later become the country's President, recalls in his memoir, *My Burma*, that some faces in the attending crowd "were radiant with happiness and joy" while other people, particularly a group of European women standing next to him, "wept copiously".

After Independence, the new government of the Union of Burma used this building and Prome Court [29] to house various ministries and government departments. The Secretariat then became known as the Ministers' Office.

PRESENT

Over the past decades, the administrative centre of power has shifted to other buildings and the Ministers' Office has fallen into disuse. In 2005, when the government moved to Nay Pyi Taw, this complex was mostly abandoned.

The Secretariat was one of five buildings selected by the Ministry of Construction to undergo basic renovation in 2011 [see Saving Yangon's Heritage, page 39]. The roofing, which had been damaged during Cyclone Nargis in 2008, was replaced with temporary fixtures. During the renovation process the majority of the roof frames, which were built of good quality teak, were found to be intact. Soil testing was also conducted and showed that the southern wing [constructed between 1889-1893] had subsided by 21 inches in the decades after it was built; though the soil appears to have stabilised since then, this has left the building with structural challenges that need to be addressed.

POTENTIAL

A full renovation of this building would be costly but it is strongly felt that the complex must be preserved due to its historical significance and national importance as the place where General Aung San and the other martyrs were killed.

In 2011, interest from Asian investors in converting the complex into a hotel was met by impassioned local resistance. Later that year, the government vetoed the plans and assured the public that the building would not be leased to hoteliers.

Suggestions for a more palatable repurposing of the former Secretariat have included a museum of colonial history that could also hold colonial and archival records and/or a general museum of Yangon history. A good model exists in the National Museum of Singapore, which has become a cultural and architectural landmark and houses a permanent exhibition of Singapore's history, and which shares a similar timeline to that of Myanmar; the building was built in 1887, at a similar time to the Secretariat, and underwent a massive three-year restoration exercise in 2003 that included a modern glass-and-steel extension.

This site is certainly large enough to support multiple uses. Architects and urban planners suggest that the southwestern section (where the Independence heroes were killed) be converted into a museum or memorial and other areas within the complex might feasibly be used to house an art centre, a cultural centre, a theatre, and/or a community hall. The addition of restaurants and shops could make the complex a key tourist attraction that would be unique in Southeast Asia.

Architect Daw Thynn Thynn Aye of Eiksietan, Co., points out the crucial trade-off between preserving heritage for the next generation and ensuring that conservation projects are financially sustainable. At the former Secretariat, she suggests starting a small-scale effort to renovate the service buildings along Anawrahta Road. These buildings, located at the northern end of the compound, are now completely derelict and have no roofing, flooring, windows, or doors. "We could start by restoring these smaller buildings," she says. "One idea might be to open them out onto the main road and convert them into shops and restaurants, or maybe even a School of Design..." For Daw Thynn Thynn Aye, and many others, the Secretariat's link to colonial governance generates no ill will: "It's our history and we can't obliterate it," she says. "Instead, we should enable the younger generation to learn from it and invite visitors to our country to learn from it, too."

BABOO NAITRAM RAMBUX

The Secretariat was constructed by a father-and-son team from Northern India. Naitram Rambux took over the family's construction company when he was just a teenager after his father was killed by a train in 1894. His father was responsible for the first wing of the Secretariat, and he erected the latter wings. Within a couple of decades he was employing thousands of workers and had become a respected member of Rangoon society, with an entry in the *Who's Who of Burma* and a 1920s guidebook stating that his "Impress on Rangoon will endure long after he and everyone in the city have passed away."

Naitram Rambux was also responsible for erecting Jubilee Hall (demolished in the early 1980s, pictured right) and the Bombay Burmah Trading Corporation (see page 117).

The President's House was completed in 1895 by Henry Hoyne-Fox in what he called a "Queen Anne Renaissance Style". It became the residence of the Governor of Burma and was the setting of many grand social functions and garden parties. Though it was luxurious, few praised its overwrought design. Lord Mountbatten, Viceroy of India after World War II, described it as "hideous" and assumed that it must have been an oversight on the part of the Royal Air Force that it wasn't bombed during the war. In the 1970s, an earthquake weakened the structure and General Ne Win, who was living there at the time, ordered it destroyed.

Jubilee Hall was constructed to commemorate Queen Victoria's Diamond Jubilee in 1897. As a public hall, it hosted various historical and cultural events. The Student Union was founded here and the building later served as a temporary mausoleum for General Aung San and his colleagues who were assassinated in the Secretariat (see page 22). In the 1940s, the British actor, Sir John Gielgud played Hamlet here and in the 1950s it was used as the National Museum. The hall was demolished in the early 1990s and is now the site of the Defense Services Museum.

2 THE PRINTING & PUBLISHING ENTERPRISE

formerly
GOVERNMENT PRESS

Location: 228 Theinbyu Road, corner of Anawrahta Road

Built: 1906-1912

Architect/ Contractor: John Begg [architect]

This large, low-rise building was built of brick and features an eclectic entranceway with dwarfed Doric columns flanking the ground-floor gate and grander double Ionic columns on the first story façade.

PAST

The Government Press came close to not being built. Though the foundations were implemented in 1906 by the government's Public Works Department, construction was halted the following year due to lack of funds. For two years the site lay idle until, in 1909, the façade was redrawn by John Begg, Consulting Architect to the Government of India. Shortly thereafter, construction was resumed. The building was finally completed in 1912 with additional amenities such as electrical lifts, stabling, and servants' quarters added the following year.

This building is built to a rectangular plan with a large internal court and was finished in brick and plaster. As stone was too costly for decoration, the building's ornamental work was cast in cement.

The Government Press was basically a distribution point for government stationery brought from India. Later, materials were printed here, including the exhaustive census reports and gazetteers through which the British catalogued their colonial possessions.

After Independence and during the socialist era, the government presses expanded into neighbouring premises on Theinbyu Road and the compound was renamed the Government Printing & Stationery Department. An entry in a government publication, marking the 14th anniversary of Independence in January 1962, describes how the building was developed from a small press and book depot into a major department with some 1,300 employees; the expansion was considered necessary to meet the increased demand of the many new ministries, government departments, boards, and corporations that emerged after Independence. Modern printing machines – using monotype, linotype, and high-speed automatic and rotary printing presses – were imported and employees were sent abroad for training at institutions such as the Melbourne School of Printing and Graphic Arts in Australia, thus enabling the office to print all the "Acts, Rules and Manuals which are essential to the government administrative machinery".

This building later served as the office of the Minister of Information and the family of the senior staff member was afforded fine residential quarters in a top-floor flat which had previously been designed as the residence of the Director of the Government Press.

PRESENT

As this building has stayed in use since it was constructed, it has been maintained in fairly good condition. However, since the press was relocated after the government moved to Nay Pyi Taw in 2005, it has only been in partial use. It is still owned by the Ministry of Information, which maintains some meeting rooms here, and the Myanmar Libraries Foundation, which was set up after Cyclone Nargis in 2008 to help restock village libraries, also occupies a few rooms.

On 45th Street, at the back of the building, the original Book Depot still stands with the inscription "Government Book Depot" above its now barred-up entrance.

POTENTIAL

Though this building has been used mostly for government printing initiatives, it has occasionally been associated with independent literary pursuits. The Myanmar Libraries Foundation encourages book donors to donate books for distribution to libraries across the country. A few years ago, the premises hosted a book fair for publishers – though a one-off event, it was popular with book sellers and buyers alike.

U Thaw Kaung, the retired Chief Librarian of the Universities Central Library, Yangon, believes the building could be converted into a splendid library. "It is in a very good location as it is downtown and easily accessible but still very quiet and peaceful," he says. "The building also has plenty of storage space and a variety of different rooms that could be used for books, periodicals, newspapers, magazines, and an electronic library."

Main façade of the old Government Press building

John Begg (1866-1937)

Consulting Architect to the Government of India

Scottish architect John Begg spent 20 years working for the colonial government in India and was responsible for many state buildings. In his designs, he strove for an aesthetic that blended both Eastern and Western styles and that would also be suited to the tropical climatic conditions. Such efforts culminated in his most famous buildings – the General Post Office, Mumbai, and the Lady Hardinge Medical College for Women at New Delhi.

According to Begg, there were two opposing schools of thought in colonial architectural theory. One school held that the British "should do in India as the Romans did in every country whereupon they planted their conquering foot", i.e., export their architectural values along with those of law and culture. The other school promoted the exclusive use of traditional indigenous architecture. Begg's own view lay between the two extremes; he believed that the modern technical skills of British architects should be combined with traditional aesthetics.

John Begg studied first at the Edinburgh Academy and later in London at the Architectural Association and The Royal Academy Schools. In 1891 he became an Associate of the Royal Institute of British Architects (ARIBA) and went on to work for a few years as a government architect in South Africa. In 1901, he was appointed Consulting Architect to the Government of Bombay and from 1908-1921 he served as Consulting Architect to the Government of India. He then returned to private practice in Edinburgh where he became head of the architectural section of Edinburgh College of Art and president of the Royal Incorporation of Architects in Scotland.

Begg Buildings in Rangoon: The Government Press (2), the Central Telegraph Office (7), and the Custom House (23).

3 BASIC EDUCATION HIGH SCHOOL 6 BOTAHTAUNG

formerly
ST. PAUL'S HIGH SCHOOL

Location: Anawrahta Road, corner of Theinbyu Road opposite the Ministers' Office

Built: 1885, with later additions

Architect/Contractor: Thomas Swales, later additions

With its wrought iron gates and sweeping driveway, this building is a prime example of a substantial 19th-century missionary school and was once part of a large mission compound that encompassed St. Mary's, the biggest Roman Catholic cathedral in Myanmar.

PAST

St. Paul's High School was founded by Bishop Paul Bigandet who served in Yangon from 1856 until his death in 1894. In 1860, Bigandet obtained the services of three De La Salle Brothers from Calcutta (now Kolkata) who were part of the Brothers of the Christian Schools, a Roman Catholic order founded in 1690 and dedicated exclusively to education. After founding St. Patrick's school in Mawlamyaing, the brothers came to Yangon and set up a school in a humble wooden building near the bishop's residence. Within just a couple of years, the school had outgrown its small premises and was moved a couple of times before finally ending up on its present site in 1885.

The original building that stands here was commissioned by Brother Valens, who is known as the "grand old man" of St. Paul's. Between 1900 and 1908, his successor, Brother O' Gregory, oversaw the addition of two new wings giving the building its current U-shape. In the 1930s, another director, Brother Patrick, added a study hall and refectory.

St. Paul's has a prestigious history. The school was one of 10 operated by the De la Salle brothers and located across the country from Mawlamyaing to Myitkyina. The street that runs in front of the school, now Anawrahta Road, was once called Bigandet Street in recognition of the school's founder and his contribution to education in Myanmar.

Lessons were taught in English and St. Paul's originally catered mostly to European and Anglo-Indian boys who were sons of British civil servants and wealthy merchants. Lim Chin Tsong, the Chinese millionaire who built the Chin Tsong Palace [30], was educated here and was one of Bigandet's favourite pupils. Among the school's many famous alumni is Deedok U Ba Cho, one of the martyrs assassinated in 1947 along with General Aung San in the Secretariat [1] across the road.

Like all missionary schools, St. Paul's High School was nationalised under the socialist government in 1965. The foreign brothers were sent home and replaced by Burmese government teachers and the school eventually became Basic Education High School 6, Botahtaung.

PRESENT

The building and grounds of St. Paul's have been well maintained. The original motto of the Brothers of the Christian Schools fraternity – *Signum Fidei* [Sign of Faith] – still exists, woven in iron into the school gates. The order's symbol, the five-pointed star of Bethlehem which led the wise men of the East to the birth of Christ, has been incorrectly rendered here as a six-pointed star.

Today, the Old Paulians' Association [founded in March 1960] unites many alumni from around the world. To be an Old Paulian, alumni must have attended the school before nationalization in 1965. The Association holds annual events within the school grounds to pay tribute to past teachers and masters, including a biannual dinner for old teachers, support for extra tutorial classes for current students, and contributions for the upkeep of buildings and school equipment. The association welcomes donations and is currently helping to update the school's science laboratory, which was built in 1922 and was the first educational laboratory in Myanmar.

"We Old Paulians support the school as much as possible," says Captain Win Than Oo, an active Old Paulian. "We have a debt of gratitude. After all, it is because of St. Paul's and the teachers who taught there that we are what we are now."

Main façade of St. Paul's High School, and wrought iron entrance gates

RANGOON 1927

Pablo Neruda

translated by Jim Potter

I came late to Rangoon.
Everything was already there:
a city
of blood,
dreams and gold,
a river that descended
from the cruel jungle
into the stifling city,
and its leprous streets
with a white hotel for whites and a gold pagoda for the golden.
All that passed
and did not pass.
Rangoon, steps wounded
by the spitters
of betel juice,
Burmese servant girls,
silk
taut against their nakedness,
as if fire accompanied
by purple tongues
were taking part in
their dance, the supreme
dance:
the dance of feet to the market,
the ballet of legs in the streets.
Supreme light that opened over my hair
a world at its zenith, it entered my eyes
and ran through my veins
into every corner of my body,
until granting me the sovereignty
of an excessive, exiled love.

A young Pablo Neruda

WORLD-FAMOUS RESIDENTS OF DALHOUSIE ROAD

Fictional home of Detective U San Sha, Myanmar's answer to Sherlock Holmes

Dalhousie Road *was once home to a poet from Chile, a fictional detective from London, and the makers of a cure-all Chinese ointment that is today sold around the world.*

The Chilean poet Pablo Neruda lived on Dalhousie [now Mahabandoola] Road from 1927-1928 when he worked at the Chilean consulate to Burma. Neruda fell in love with a Burmese woman he called Josie Bliss who poetry critics would later identify as his most important muse. As Neruda describes her, Bliss was an incredibly jealous woman and used to brandish a knife at him when she suspected his infidelity. He ended up escaping to Ceylon [now Sri Lanka] but Bliss managed to track him down and camped out on his front lawn, mournfully playing the Paul Robeson records they had once enjoyed listening to together. Josie Bliss disappeared during World War II and, though Neruda later returned and tried to find her, he lost touch with her forever. Even in later life, the memory of Josie Bliss continued to haunt his poetry.

The address of the Chilean consulate – #295 Dalhousie Road – no longer exists. The building it was housed in was torn down shortly after Neruda fled and was replaced by the Haroon Soorty Mansions, at the southern side of the Secretariat.

When the Burmese writer and translator Shwe U Daung [1889-1973] adapted Arthur Conan Doyle's famous Sherlock Holmes detective stories for a Burmese audience in the 1930s, he dressed the British sleuth in a *longyi* and renamed him Detective U San Sha. He set his home and office a couple blocks down from Dalhousie at #58 on 40th Street, making this address the equivalent of the famous London address 221b, Baker Street [in London, 221b Baker Street is now a museum dedicated to the fictional sleuth that features his bedroom and study, furnished just as they are in the stories]. The Yangon building still stands, tucked away behind the Armenian Church and between some old warehouses. In the fictional world, U San Sha and U Thein Maung, Dr. Watson's Burmese counterpart, used to climb onto the flat roof in the evenings and sit debating the details of each case with the Yangon skyline spread out around them.

Dalhousie Road is also the origin of an analgesic ointment that became a global phenomenon still known and sold around the world today. In 1870, the Chinese herbalist Aw Chu Kin moved to Yangon and opened an apothecary called Eng Aun Tong, the Hall of Eternal Peace. Later, two of his sons took over the business, establishing an office at the far eastern end of Dalhousie Road. One of the sons, Boon Par ("Gentle Leopard"), apprenticed himself to a local pharmacist called U Thaw, who bequeathed to the young man a secret recipe for a balm that could relieve all manner of pain; his only proviso was that if the recipe made money some of the proceeds should be donated to charity. Boon Par refined the ointment while his brother, Boon Haw ("Gentle Tiger"), sought clever ways to promote it. They packaged it in tiny jars, called it Ban Kim Ewe ("Ten Thousand Golden Oil"), and used their family Hakka connections to convince Chinese medicine shops to stock the balm. Later, the packaging was decorated with the image of a snarling tiger and the ointment was re-branded as tiger balm.

By 1920, Boon Haw was considered one of the wealthiest Chinese businessmen in the country. The brothers kept their promise to the late pharmacist who had given them the original recipe. The *Who's Who of Burma*, 1927, notes that Boon Haw "is of the most charitable nature but does not advertise the good he has done for many of his countrymen; during the past three years he has repatriated 784 aged [Chinese] people at his own expense, not only paying their passage but giving each one ten dollars and some tiger balm". Among many other donations (he endeavored to spend 40 percent of his net income on charity) is the Aw Boon Haw & Aw Boon Par Memorial Hall, which is still standing in the Yangon School for the Blind and has been used as an orphanage school.

Towards the end of the decade, the brothers moved the headquarters of their expanding business to Singapore. They did not forget their Burmese origins and later sponsored a pavilion at the Thanboddhay Pagoda near Monywa, northwest of Mandalay, where statues of the two brothers are depicted barefooted and gazing at a colourful frieze of roaring tigers.

B AROUND SULE PAGODA

Sule Pagoda marks the architectural and spiritual heart of downtown Yangon. It is the centrifugal point from which the original city plan emanates. The plan, drawn up in the 1850s after the second Anglo-Burmese War by a Scottish engineer called Lieutenant Alexander Fraser, was based on an earlier mapping of the city that proposed a chessboard pattern of narrow streets running north-south intersected by wide boulevards running east-west to form a grid along the riverside with the Sule Pagoda as its centre.

During British times, this neighbourhood combined high-end commercial buildings with heavy-duty public offices, and it is still thought of as the central business district. The most imposing edifice is **City Hall (4)**, a unique and symbolic building that marks the first blending of British architecture and traditional Myanmar design. Next to City Hall is the former **Immigration Department (5)**, which was originally built in 1910 to house Rowe & Company, a shopping emporium that remained Burma's best department store for nearly half a century. Diagonally across the pagoda is another former department store that later served as the **Ministry of Hotels & Tourism (6)**. Further down Mahabandoola Garden Street is the **High Court (8)**, and around the corner on Mahabandoola Road is the **Central Telegraph Office (7)**

Under the British, Mahabandoola Garden was known as Fytche Square after Sir Albert Fytche (Chief Commissioner, 1867-1871) and a white marble statue of Queen Victoria stood in the centre of the gardens. Queen Victoria is, of course, long gone and in her place stands the obelisk and surrounding structures of the Independence memorial designed by the Burmese sculptor U Ohn Kyaing and erected in 1950 to commemorate the end of colonial rule. Mahabandoola Road and Garden are named after the 19th-century General Mahabandoola who died in action and is celebrated for his resistance against British rule; he conquered Assam and led the Burmese army against the East India Company in 1824.

Today, the Sule Pagoda roundabout is a busy intersection due mostly to a bus depot situated opposite City Hall. Architecturally, it is still a spectacular setting surrounded on all sides by impressive and sizeable heritage buildings.

SAVING YANGON'S HERITAGE

In 2010, the following five buildings were selected by the Ministry of Construction's Department of Human Settlement and Housing Development to undergo basic renovation: the Ministers' Office or old Secretariat (1), the former Immigration Office (5), the former Ministry of Hotels & Tourism (6), the Myanmar Oil & Gas Enterprise (10), and the Myanmar Export & Import Corporation. The effort also involved the contributed expertise of the Association of Myanmar Architects, the Myanmar Engineering Society, and private contractors. Architects and engineers drew plans of each building and assessed the structure and stability, cataloguing strengths and weaknesses. The actual renovation work was conducted with a limited budget and within a very short timescale (January-March 2011) and consisted mostly of basic weather protection measures to ensure that the buildings do not deteriorate further in their unoccupied state.

4 CITY HALL

Location: Mahabandoola Road, corner of Sule Pagoda Road

Built: 1925-1940

Architect/ Contractor: L. A. McClumpha, A. G. Bray, and Sithu U Tin (architects), Clark & Greig and A. C. Martin & Co. (contractor)

City Hall is an enormous four-storey edifice located in the very centre of downtown Yangon. This unique structure was the first large-scale masonry building to combine European design and engineering technology with traditional Myanmar flourishes.

PAST

In 1886, the city's municipal authority purchased Ripon Hall, a community dance hall located on the site of the present-day City Hall. The dance hall was converted for use as a municipal headquarters but, as the city expanded, so did the needs of the municipal offices, and additional space had to be rented in one of the top floors of the neighbouring department store, Rowe & Company (5). In 1903, the municipality purchased the land behind Ripon Hall to build an extension but it later became apparent that an entirely new building was needed; the original hall was condemned by the Health Department for being structurally unsound and overrun with "plague-infested" rats (a serious consideration given that plague outbreaks killed over 2,460 people in the city in 1905 and over 1,050 in 1908, according to a city Health Department report referenced in *Twentieth Century Impressions of Burma*).

Plans were laid to construct a larger building that would reflect the city's growing importance as a regional trading hub and capital city. In 1913, the Municipal Committee held a design competition for which it set the oddly humble mandate of a building with "some pretensions to architectural beauty".

Over 30 entries were assessed by Henry Seton-Morris, then Consulting Architect to the Government of Burma. Of the winning design drawn by L. A. McClumpha he wrote, "I have no hesitation inawarding this design the first place. It stands alone in its grasp of the ventilation problem which has baffled the authors of so many fine designs. In proportion, in restraint, in dignity, the Municipal Offices and Public Hall when built will be the finest group of architectural buildings in Burma."

The following year, however, World War I broke out and the plans were shelved. Due to the resulting economic and bureaucratic constraints, construction did not begin until over a decade later in 1925. By then, nationalist sentiment was growing more organised and it was demanded that the building incorporate Burmese architectural features. Burmese politician U Ba Pe gave a rousing speech at the Burma Legislative Council, calling for a new design for City Hall that would feature the ornamentations of the ancient capital Bagan [formerly Pagan]. When European members of the Council disagreed with the use of religious-inspired architecture for a civic building, U Ba Pe responded, "No civic architecture in the world can be found that is not founded on either ecclesiastical, monumental or other religious architecture." He won the debate and the Burmese architect Sithu U Tin [1883-1972] was selected for the job of reimagining City Hall.

U Tin had made a name for himself through his elegant design for the popular Burmese Pavilion at the Wembley Exhibition held in London in 1924. Having worked in the Public Works Department and been apprenticed to an engineering firm in Mumbai [then Bombay], he would later be remembered as one of Myanmar's first architects. The end result of his design for City Hall took on palatial form, featuring three-tiered *pyatthat* roofing and traditional Myanmar iconography such as peacocks and *nagas* [serpents].

Side view of the newly painted City Hall

As with the Secretariat, construction was conducted in stages. The north wing was erected first (notice the external guttering pipes on the back wall, dated 1925) by the building firm, Clark & Greig. The following year, architect A. G. Bray (ARIBA) who was manager of United Engineers' Yangon branch, oversaw the design process of successive wings. Construction was carried out by A. C. Martin & Co., which was run by a highly experienced Persian contractor from Iran who had laid most of the modern asphalt roads in Yangon. Construction progressed anti-clockwise and the final wing to be built was the section facing Mahabandoola Garden Street, which was not completed until 1940. An annual municipal report proudly stated, "The building is worthy of the metropolis and inaugurates a new era in secular Burmese architecture."

This building has remained in use as City Hall until the present day. During the 1950s, it was the city's largest auditorium and hosted weddings, concerts, and other ceremonies. In the 1970s, the National Library was housed here on the second floor.

PRESENT

This building is occupied by the city's current municipal authorities, the Yangon City Development Committee (YCDC).

The building's exterior was for many years a creamy tangerine colour that became stained with dark patches of mildew. In mid-2011, it was repainted a strikingly luminous lilac with purple finishes.

At the back entrance it is still possible to see the original insignia on the iron gates, which reads Municipal Corporation of Rangoon (in British times City Hall was referred to simply as "the Corporation").

Though local architects appreciate the building's historic significance, its architectural contribution is debatable: "It's an iconic building for us in Yangon, like the Eiffel Tower is to Paris," says architect U Sun Oo, Vice President of the Association of Myanmar Architects. "But whether it has architectural value or not I can not say. The Burmese additions were made after the basic plan had already been decided so there was no strong conceptual structure underpinning the design. In stylistic terms, it is certainly unique; I would call it 'Classical Revival', a recomposing of the old ornaments and components of Burmese palace and temple architecture."

British-Myanmar Style

The design flourishes on City Hall were created by Burmese architect Sithu U Tin and were inspired by the ancient capital of Bagan. Other examples of buildings that incorporate this unique hybrid style are Basic Education High School 2 Dagon (formerly Myoma School) and the Yangon Railway Station, which was rebuilt in this style after being bombed during in World War II.

City Hall immediately after World War II, with bomb damage to the High Court building visible in the foreground, Glenn S. Hensley, 1945.

5 FORMER IMMIGRATION DEPARTMENT

formerly
ROWE & CO. DEPARTMENT STORE

Location: 416 Mahabandoola Road, corner of Mahabandoola Garden Street

Built: 1908-1910

Architect/ Contractor: Charles F. Stevens (architect), Robinson & Mundy (contractor)

Once dubbed the "Harrods of the East", this building was designed to be the country's fanciest department store. With its corner tower, black-and-white marble floors, and top-floor balconettes, the structure still retains hints of its former opulence.

PAST

Throughout British rule, Rowe & Company was one of the principal retail firms in Myanmar. Founded in the mid 1860s by Mr. R. V. Rowe, the company began business in a small premise on Mogul (now Shwebontha) Street selling drapery and general goods. The shop was moved several times before finally locating in its prominent premises off Fytche Square (now Mahabandoola Garden).

This building was designed by a well-known architectural firm from Mumbai, Messrs. Charles F. Stevens & Co. Charles Stevens was the son of Frederick W. Stevens, who designed the Victoria Terminus in Mumbai, an elaborate building that is widely acknowledged as one of the most magnificent examples of colonial architecture.

In his design for Rowe & Co., the younger Stevens made use of all the latest engineering techniques. Covering some 22,000 square feet, the building featured the city's first basement and a steel framework. The interior was described at the time as being "fitted up in the most modern style" and no expense was spared on conveniences; though electricity had only just been introduced to Yangon around the time of its construction, the store sported the city's earliest electric lifts and ceiling fans.

Rowe & Co. department store, circa 1950s

The local contractor commissioned for the construction job was Messrs. Robinson & Mundy, a reputable firm of civil engineers, architects, and builders that had been established in Yangon since 1870. Robinson & Mundy were responsible for many high-profile commercial buildings in the city, some of which are still standing; namely, the J. & F. Graham Shipping Company [19] and Finlay, Fleming & Company [10] offices.

Europeans and wealthy Asians flocked to Rowe & Co. for luxury, as well as practical and imported, goods. Four times a year, the store issued a 300-page illustrated catalogue that featured "ladies' & gentlemen's outfitting, drapery, millinery, boots and shoes, crockery and glassware, brassware trunks, cutlery, watches and clocks, and saddlery". The store's bicycle department was known for importing the world's top models. Rowe & Co. also operated 38 smaller branches across the country.

Building details, Rowe & Co. (RC) department store

During World War II, the department store was thoroughly looted. British civil servant E. C. V. Foucar was appalled to note that even British soldiers strolled in to take their pick of the goods available; in his memoir *I Lived in Burma*, Foucar wrote that an officer was spotted one evening emerging from the store with a fine golf bag bulging with an equally excellent selection of clubs. Despite its wartime losses, Rowe & Co. managed to rebuild its assets and reopen for business after the war. In the 1950s, it was still favoured by those who could afford it. A Shan princess recalls in her memoirs, "I loved going to Rowe's. Here one was still served by Britishers [as British people were called in India and Myanmar] behind the counters, and Rowe's proud boast was that there was nothing in the world that could not be bought from them. If they did not have it, Rowe's would obtain it wherever it came from." She went so far as to compare it to London's most famous department store and called it, "a veritable Harrods of the East".

Rowe & Co. stayed in business during the early 1960s but was nationalised along with all its branches and over 12,200 trading establishments throughout Myanmar in April 1964. During the socialist period one section of the building served as a library for the Worker's College and it was later taken over by the Department of Immigration & Manpower.

PRESENT

The Department of Immigration & Manpower has since been relocated and the building now stands empty. On the Mahabandoola Garden Street side, weeds have grown among the brickwork and damp has spread along the exposed plumbing but the initials "RC" can still be seen inscribed beneath a high gabled window.

The building was one of five heritage structures chosen for renovation by the Ministry of Construction [see Saving Yangon's Heritage, page 39]. As the roof was badly damaged during Cyclone Nargis in 2008, the architects and engineers who assessed the building decided to remove the entire roof and replace it with temporary metal sheeting because it was judged that the existing structure would no longer be able to stand the weight of the original clay tiles.

POTENTIAL

The older generation has fond memories of the Rowe & Co. department store as a reminder of more glamorous times, and the building is often photographed by tourists. As the neighbourhood in which this building stands is still predominately a commercial one, it is most obviously suited to being used as a department store or premises for other business that would benefit from being located in the heart of the city.

Even-4 by Maung Khine Mar (MKM), Acrylic, 2011

This is the last in a series of four 38x24-inch canvases inspired by the juxtapositions between old and new structures in Yangon. Maung Khine Mar was born in Sittwe in 1980 and this painting was part of a group show held at the Lokanat Gallery [pages 83-84] in November 2011.

6 FORMER MINISTRY OF HOTELS & TOURISM

Location: 77-91 Sule Pagoda Road, corner of Mahabandoola Road

Built: circa 1905

Architect/ Contractor: Thomas Swales

In its various guises as a department store, magazine office, post-war supplies office, and government ministry, this building has remained at the centre of Yangon's physical and cultural development.

PAST

Originally commissioned by an Indian merchant, the building was leased in 1918 to U Ba Nyunt, a wealthy Burmese businessman who transformed it into the city's first Burmese-owned department store known as Myanmar Aswe, or "Burmese Favourite". U Ba Nyunt housed his family on the top floor of the premises and operated the department store on the lower floors. The store was popular with Burmese but he struggled to compete with Rowe & Co. [5] on the other side of Sule Pagoda. As Rowe & Co. was a British-run store, it benefited from tax exemptions on imported goods and was able to under-price Myanmar Aswe.

In 1920, U Ba Nyunt used the building as offices for the newly established *Dagon* [the ancient name for Yangon] magazine, one of the earliest magazines in Myanmar. The building soon became a gathering point for aspiring writers and the magazine served as the starting point for a number of famous authors, some of whom later added "Dagon" to their pen name. These include Dagon Taya, whose extract is featured in this book on pages 58-61, as well as Burma's first female novelist, Dagon Khin Khin Lay [1904-1981], who later founded the Burma Women Writers Association, and Dagon Shwe Hmyar [1895-1982], who went on to write popular mystery and adventure stories and was much-loved for his translations of the British novelist Rider Haggard. Other *Dagon* contributors who began their careers here include the pioneering writer Theippan Maung Wa [1899-1942], whose experimental short stories began a trend that eschewed traditionally ornate literary prose and made reading available to the common man, and Khin Myo Chit [1915-1999], who later became known for her short stories, journalism, and English language books celebrating Burmese culture. The prolific writer P. Monin [1883-1940], whose self-help books are still best sellers today, was run over on his bicycle as he was leaving the building in 1940 and later died in Yangon General Hospital [26].

BURMESE FAVOURITE

The Leading Burmese Firm

LIST OF DEPARTMENTS

BURMESE FAVOURITE CO.

In the guide Seaports of the Far East (1924), *the Burmese Favourite department store housed in this building is described as the city's leading local merchandiser:*

"Their large and handsome establishment has a length of 200 feet, and its appointments and entire ensemble form a harmony of artistic adaptation and utility that admits the display of the stock in a very pleasing and effective manner throughout its twelve departments.

Nowhere in Rangoon can be found a more comprehensive assortment of silk goods – the entire East is there represented in all its varieties of the most charming materials in every colour possible to silk production.

The firm specialises in Burmese coat making, and also turns out suits cut in the latest and most approved English fashions, for which they have always been at the disposal of their customers, a comprehensive assortment of high-quality tweeds, taffetas, flannels, and tropical suiting.

Particularly noteworthy is the department for boots and shoes, with its extensive variety of footwear including all manner of Burmese sandals and slippers, and also the Signet All-American Beacon shoes, Dr. Sawyers' cushion shoes, and Whitehouse shoes, for which the firm are agents."

U Ba Nyunt also set up one of the first Burmese film companies in this building, called A1 film company. During the 1930s, various other businesses were located here. Old directories list the following: W. H. Minis Estate Agents, Dodge & Seymour Ltd., Dagoun Photographic Studio, and Arya Nivas Hindu Lodge (advertised as "the only and the most popular" boarding house for vegetarians in the city).

After World War II, this building was requisitioned by the government. The British authorities made use of its central location and commodious space as a Civil Supply Board to distribute post-war rations. In 1964, the building housed the Ministry of Trade Cooperative No. 3 and No. 20 (in charge of Food and Beverage respectively) and functioned as a staff shop where civil servants could purchase subsid sed supplies.

Later, in the 1970s, the Tourism Burma office moved into the building and was responsible for arranging limited travel and hotel vouchers for the handful of foreign tourists able to visit the country during the socialist era. In 1992, as Myanmar prepared for the possibility of increased tourism under a more open economic system, the building was taken over by the newly established Ministry of Hotels & Tourism.

PRESENT

After its many decades of varied activity, the building fell into disuse when the government moved to the new capital in Nay Pyi Taw at the end of 2005. It was one of five buildings chosen for renovation by the Ministry of Construction [see Saving Yangon's Heritage, page 39]. The roof was badly damaged during Cyclone Nargis in 2008 and needed emergency repairs as the top floor was threatened by exposure. The basic renovations involved new roofing and damp protection.

POTENTIAL

Members of the Association of Myanmar Architects [AMA] feel that preserving this building is key to the architectural integrity of the Sule Pagoda roundabout, which is surrounded by heritage buildings. Though there is talk of repurposing the building as a hotel, architects who worked on the basic renovation suggest that the space and structure provided by the building would be more appropriate for a downtown office building that boasts a prime and historic location.

clockwise:
Shwe Hmyar
Khin Myo Chit
Theippan Maung Wa
P Monin
Khin Kin Lay

7 CENTRAL TELEGRAPH OFFICE

Location: 125-133 Pansodan Street, corner of Mahabandoola Road

Built: 1913-1917

Architect/ Contractor: John Begg (architect), Clark & Greig (contractor)

This functional and imposing, if not overtly beautiful, structure is a classic example of administrative colonial architecture. Its main entrance is dominated by an oversized portico with coupled Ionic columns and open-bed pediments.

PAST

This building was the last to be designed by John Begg, Consulting Architect to the Government of India, for Yangon. It was designed as a four-storey, steel-framed building with brick walls between stanchions placed at 20-foot intervals. During early excavation work, the contractor discovered that part of the plot was severely waterlogged and innovative methods were used to remedy the situation. Piles 9 inches in diameter were sunk across the swampy area and filled with sand. The sand was stirred for days until it became firm and dry. The entire site was then levelled with more sand and covered with 2.5 inches of fine cement.

At the time of its construction, the Telegraph Office offered Yangon residents the technological wonder of speedy communications with the rest of the world, and this building has always been associated with information travelling into and out of the country.

Not long after the Japanese captured Yangon in World War II, the new authorities issued an order for city residents to bring their radios to the Telegraph Office to have them converted so they would be unable to receive Allied news broadcasts from India. After months passed and the radios were not returned, it was

Building details, including a current brass plaque

surmised that the authorities had used the announcement as a ruse to confiscate private wireless sets and prevent any news of the war from spreading through Yangon.

In the 1950s, after Independence, this building was still the only agency handling foreign cables, with about 96,000 outgoing and 87,000 incoming messages sent per year. The Telegraph Office continued to serve its purpose as a link to the outside world during the socialist period and, throughout the 1990s and early 2000s, was still favoured by city residents for its reliable domestic telephone lines and international fax services.

PRESENT

Today, other communication technologies have superseded the usefulness of the Telegraph Office. The building is owned by the Ministry of Communications, Posts & Telegraphs, and the ground floor is currently being used as a telephone mall, with stalls selling mobile phones and SIM cards.

Diagonally across the intersection, on the northeast corner, is a colourful building housing various shops that include the Kyaw Home Mart. This was formerly the Tejoomal Building, an emporium of oriental curios that sold a wide selection of silverware, silks, and carvings from across Asia.

8 HIGH COURT

Location: 89-123 Pansodan Street, with an entrance on Mahabandoola Garden Street

Built: 1905-1911

Architect/ Contractor: James Ransome (architect), Bagchi & Co. (contractor)

The dusky rose-coloured High Court is another outstanding example of a grand old building of Empire. Built in the Queen Anne style, it includes characteristic features such as rooftop lion statues and a bell clock tower that once rang out the hour.

PAST

"Nothing caught the spirit of the Victorian Empire better than the idea of legal majesty, embodied in India [and Myanmar] as in England in the presence of grave judges and still graver buildings," wrote Jan Morris, a popular historian of the British Empire. In her book *Stones of Empire*, she describes how British courts in the colonies were designed to intimidate: "The High Courts did not often express a quality of mercy, but generally made the malefactor feel as alarmed as the judge was all confident."

This building is, as Morris describes, an archetypal colonial administrative building – large and imposing. The lion statues, crouched above the Pansodan Street façade, symbolise Great Britain and the regal might of its Empire. As the Indian architect Manish Chakraborti, head of the Kolkata-based firm Continuity which specialises in the preservation of historic buildings, observed, "The British in India and Burma built as if they were going to be here forever."

The land for this building was purchased in 1900 but construction did not begin until five years later after several plans had been perused and rejected. Finally, one of the designs proposed by James Ransome (1865-1944), Consulting Architect to the Government of India, was chosen.

CLARK & GREIG

Clark & Greig, the Yangon-based contractor that took on the job of building the Telegraph Office, was first established in Yangon in 1910. The firm is highlighted in Seaports of the Far East, 1924:

"In nothing is the influence of Messrs. Clark & Greig, Ltd., better demonstrated than by their exemplification of the advantages of armoured-tubular flooring in the many buildings which they have erected and in the new ones on which they are engaged. The armoured-tubular system solves the problem of constructing floors and roofs without the use of any centring.

A considerable portion of the firm's new premises is devoted to the manufacture of the webs and tubes; and, as these are set and matured when delivered to the buildings, entire floors can be assembled in the simplest possible manner and with such rapidity that they can be used by workmen of other trades on the day after the top layer has been laid. The consequent omission of steel girders effects a great savings of steel work and corresponding diminution of risk in case of fire.

Messrs. Clark & Greig, Ltd., also specialise in every description of decorative and structural steel work.

The firm's telegraphic address is 'Concrete, Rangoon'".

Views of the High Court today

opposite: The High Court circa 1900, view from across Fytche Square

The latest innovations in engineering were put to good use in the building's construction. In Yangon's swampy soil, the clock tower was a risky endeavour and required extensive foundations made of *thitya*, a hardwood that is especially durable in damp conditions. To stabilise the tower without jeopardising the surrounding building, *thitya* logs of 15-18 inches in diameter were driven into the soil at 3-foot intervals and it was constructed with a clean slipjoint all around.

The work was executed by the Indian-owned construction firm Bagchi & Co., which was also involved in another important contract to construct Yangon General Hospital [26]. To maintain the quality of their constructions, Bagchi & Co. made their own bricks and ran a brick factory producing 10 million bricks each year. The architect Ransome observed that brick buildings in India had a colour very different to those at home and speculated it was down to the distinct hue of the local brick, which he described as a "pale crushed strawberry" colour.

The building was fitted with state-of-the-art fixtures. The newly established British Plumbing and Sanitary Engineering Co., which was the only firm of its kind in the country at the time, installed modern plumbing and toilet facilities. Electricity had only just been introduced to Yangon, and the building was wired by the electrical firm Stewart, Raeburn & Co. using techniques recently acquired in Manchester, England.

PRESENT

Like the neighbouring Telegraph Office, these courts have been in almost constant use for their original purpose and remain in relatively good condition, both internally and externally. Since the Supreme Court was reestablished in the new capital of Nay Pyi Taw, this building is no longer the highest court in Myanmar and is now only partially occupied.

IN THE WORDS OF THE ARCHITECTS

Though James Ransome and his successor as Consulting Architect to the Government of India, John Begg, agreed that colonial architecture should incorporate the traditional aesthetics of its locale, they were not always able to actualise their visions. When John Begg saw the High Court nearing completion during his 1909 visit to Yangon, he was unimpressed:

"There is no use affecting a great liking for it though it is of a type design fairly characteristic of modern India. Bombay is full of it, Calcutta is fast filling, and it has even crept into the schools of art. But it is of such a nature as to tempt the architect to say unkind things of it, the more so as it receives a certain amount of popular admiration. It has not the art which conceals art, nor the simplicity and dignity that should characterise a hall of justice. It is somewhat over-designed."

Years later, at a talk in London, James Ransome explained the difficulties he had to labour under when designing such buildings:

"Some months after my arrival in India, I was instructed not to put up any mongrel buildings [which blended British and local designs]. Calcutta should be Classic, Bombay Gothic, Madras Saracenic, Rangoon Renaissance and so on. I have never regretted these instructions, as they forced upon me a task I should not otherwise have undertaken – that of attempting to adapt each of the known styles of architecture to our requirements in India, an attempt which confined me in my suspicion that one and all were unsuited to the purpose."

MAY
by *Dagon Taya*, an extract

Dagon Taya [born 1919] is one of Myanmar's most prominent writers. This is an extract from May *[published in 1941], a novel he adapted from the English novel* Self *by John Beverley Nichols. This extract finds May, the troubled heroine, taking a nighttime stroll through downtown Yangon. Set in the 1930s, it brings to life an area in which many of the buildings covered in this book are located. Dagon Taya himself took his pen name from* Dagon *magazine, which was first published in the former Ministry of Hotels & Tourism [6] building.*

Cars, lorries, and rickshaws are going to and fro on the road. You can hear the snack sellers calling, children singing, and the noise of laughter and chatter from the room next door. The gruelling sound of R.E.T [Rangoon Electric Tramway] carriages can also be heard on Dalhousie Road [now Mahabandoola]. These are the sounds of downtown Yangon. May is looking at the road down below, sticking her torso out the window but she does not hear any of these sounds; she is immersed deep in her thoughts.

May vaguely recalls wiping the blood off her mouth with a towel after receiving the money from U Bay Maung in his room. Even now, her cheek still feels the pain a little bit. Mentally, it was so painful that she had thought about tearing up all the money. She cried while packing her stuff, brooding over the harassment, and left Bago in the morning. Daw Nyein Khin would be so happy to see her leave. U Bay Maung was still in bed, with the excuse that he had a headache. Hnin and Win, however, were really sad to see their teacher leave. They walked her all the way to the gate of the compound. She could remember vividly the walk from the house to the railway station; the smell of the rice paddies was strong in the wind, and the flowers smelled so lovely. From then on, she stopped thinking.

Yesterday she was in Bago, now she is in Yangon. All the way from Bago [formerly Pegu] to Yangon she pondered where to go, watching the paddy fields pass slowly by. The only thing she knew for sure was that she wanted to wander around Yangon for a couple of days. She would consider going to Ma Khin Si's place and applying for a teaching position somewhere only after she had wandered around the city. She had already sent a letter by the morning post to Ma Khin Si saying that she would be coming over. May is staying at the YWCA guest house in Yangon. She is now by herself, with no guardian, and she can do whatever she pleases. She tries to guess what people in Bago would think of her leaving; the upper-class women will be truly happy to see the back of her, she imagines.

Freedom is now hers. She needs to go to Ma Khin Si's place and get ahold of Ma Kin Si's brother, Kyaw Myint. The fact that Kyaw Myint received 1800 *kyat* from his grandmother has not escaped her mind. That money, earned from profits made in the rice trade, was given to him well before his grandmother's death. If she can make Kyaw Myint hers, she knows she will be able to live comfortably in Yangon.

Suddenly, May shrugs her shoulders. She will be in the middle of Ma Khin Si's family in a day or two. Before that, she wants to ramble around town. Yangon is her kind of town. She can see it from her window. Yangon is crammed with tall buildings, cars, trams, cinemas, and parks. Yangon can offer her a multitude of colours, music, passion, and love. May's thoughts have no direction, it seems.

May glances at her watch and sees that is five minutes to six. She decides to take a stroll downtown. She checks herself in the mirror, puts on quite a lot of perfume, applies her lipstick, and dabs a little bit of hair cream on her curly hair. Flinging the grey coat that was a present from Ma Khin Si over her shoulder, she saddles up her shoes, goes downstairs, and hails a rickshaw.

On her way downtown, seeing people on the streets, she feels cheered as she watches them move about in all directions. Couples are making their way in rickshaws and motor cars. The rickshaw she is in turns into Sparks Street [now Bo Aung Kyaw Street], and then heads west along Montgomerie [now Bogyoke Aung San Road]. The place is packed with people and vehicles as the movies have just finished. The bright lights seem to be coming from everywhere.

May is now close to the railway station where crowds are milling in front of the Star and Olympia cinemas. She passes through the intersection of Sule Pagoda Road and Montgomerie Street. She asks the rickshaw man to stop in front of the Continental Building. She can see the flickering lights from advertisements atop the flyover bridge – Tiger Soda, Polo Cigarettes, and a few beer and alcohol names.

May gazes at the people walking by. People are shuffling rapidly past the English cinemas – the Globe, Pladium, and Odeon. The motorcars, horse carts, and rickshaws are crowded so thick that the police have to intervene. May used to come around this area quite often when she was at the Diocesan Teachers' Training College. You have to pass through here to go to the movies, or when you go to Scott Market. It is a beautiful place at night with the colourful lights. Men are staring at her. "Wow, that's a cool chick!" say some, albeit indistinctly.

May considers watching a movie but brushes aside the idea immediately; it would be too boring. She crosses the street towards the Savoy Bakery. The red colour from the lights of the GEC Radio Building seems to intensify her beauty. And she walks on towards to Sule Pagoda. When she glances at the Piccadilly, she sees a young couple walking down the stairs; they are all smiles and holding each other's hands. They must be newlyweds. As they get into a rickshaw, the young man slips his arm around the woman's waist. May can hear the young woman say, "No, there are a lot of people around..."

"Well, this is Yangon," May thinks to herself. And that is indeed Yangon, just as she thinks. She crosses Fraser Street [now Anawrahta Road]. The night market is full of bright lights, noises from Indian street sellers, and the smell of frying oil from the *paratha* [fried flat-bread] stalls. It's like a festival with all these people and vehicles around.

May happens to be in front of the Roselin Milk Shop, and she steps in to have a cup of milk. There are two Englishmen and an Englishwoman inside the shop.

Now she arrives in front of the Municipal Town Hall [today known as City Hall [4]]. She realises that she has not watched the Burmese *anyeint* of dance and comedy at Fytche Square [now Mahabandoola Garden Park] opposite Town Hall in a long time. She is tempted by the audience's laughter and cheers to the jokes from the comedians. She doesn't try to resist the temptation and walks over to the other side of the road. She is in a happy mood now. She likes the crowdedness around her, and searches for a nice spot to watch the show.

"May! May!"

She has to stop searching because of someone yelling behind her. A young woman runs towards her and grabs her hand. It is her old friend, Than Kyi, a classmate from the Diocesan College.

"Hey Mabel!" May calls her by the name she used during their college days.

Than Kyi asks her about all kinds of topics without stopping. May matches her with questions. As it turns out, Than Kyi has separated from her husband.

"Are you alone, May?"

"Yes, how about you?"

"My friends are there."

May looks and sees two guys between 20 and 23 years of age wearing brown woollen jackets. They are talking to each other, smoking cigarettes. May tries to figure out the connection between the two guys and Than Kyi. Her friend sports bright red colour on her lips, cheeks, and nails. Her hair is also curled. And she talks in a livelier manner than when she was in college. She looks like she knows what she is doing.

"Where are you at now?" Than Kyi's question interrupts her drifting thoughts.

"Well, in Yangon I should say. I spent quite some time in Bago though."

"I see..."

The dancer on the stage is dancing with her chest held high. The two comedians are now searching for jokes. It is a sizable audience. There are Indians, Chinese, monks, women, men, young people and old, and enemies and friends. The cool breeze is gently blowing through a night that still is young. The High Court [8], Reserve Bank [now Myawaddy Bank [9]], Sule Pagoda, and the Town Hall are surrounding the park as if they are guarding it. This is not the countryside where the cuckoos and the doves make music. This is not an elegant rural area where flowers and trees fill the air with fragrance. This is, in fact, where noise is in ample supply from all the carriages and people. This is where the air is filled with the smell from people. In the past, May used to come here in the evenings to get some fresh air. She observes the surroundings as she chats with Than Kyi. There are surely many men who covet her blue eyes. But she doesn't care, she wants better...

C MERCHANT ROAD, THE BANKING QUARTERS

Together with the lower block of Pansodan Street this stretch of Merchant Road, which intersects with Sule Pagoda Road, was and still is the city's banking hub. The grandiose **Myawaddy Bank (9)** building dominates the scene, while other **Merchant Road banks (11)** in heritage buildings include the First Private Bank, Innwa Bank, and a branch of the Myanmar Foreign Trade Bank, which occupies the old Hong Kong and Shanghai Banking Corporation headquarters. The section of Merchant Road to the west of Sule Pagoda Road is undergoing considerable development with a number of new office blocks recently built and currently under construction. There, tucked between two modern high-rises, is the **Myanmar Oil & Gas Enterprise (10)**, formerly the powerful and profitable Burmah Oil Company.

9 MYAWADDY BANK

formerly
RESERVE BANK OF INDIA

Location: 24/26 Sule Pagoda Road, corner of Merchant Road

Built: 1939

Architect/ Contractor: G. Douglas Smart, Palmer & Turner (architect)

This monumental cut-stone edifice is a unique example of neoclassical-inspired architecture in Yangon – its size and grandeur are emblematic of the country's economic potential before World War II.

PAST

This building was originally designed to house the Reserve Bank of India, which had become the British colonial government's primary bank and was responsible for the issuance of bank notes in India and Myanmar. Even after Myanmar separated from India in 1937, the Reserve Bank continued to manage the country's financial system.

World War II brought dramatic upheavals for Myanmar's banking community. In the early months of 1942, as the Japanese army advanced towards Yangon, staff at the Reserve Bank of India sought to prevent money from falling into Japanese hands. Deposits were kept to a minimum and employees were under orders to take any remaining balance with them when they evacuated; in the event that they were unable to carry it all, they were instructed to burn the banknotes and jettison coins into the river or sea.

When the Japanese army arrived in Yangon in March 1942, soldiers entered this building and attempted to plunder the Reserve Bank's vaults. Unable to open the Chubb safe doors, they blasted a hole in the vault's wall only to find it empty. Bank staff had already managed to get the safe's contents to northern Myanmar where A. K. Potter, the bank's Controller of Finance, took responsibility for disposing of remaining currency that couldn't be carried onwards. Potter took the coins down to the river by ox cart, loaded them onto a motorboat, and scattered them in a deepwater channel. The banknotes were harder to dispose of as they would not burn easily. Potter and his colleagues hit on the idea of creating small furnaces by piling bricks of banknotes into hollow domes; using crumpled notes as tinder, they dropped the flaming money inside each dome. The fires burned throughout the night and records show that bank staff managed to destroy over 350 million rupees.

Later that year, the Japanese war-time government established the People's Bank of Burma in this building and issued Southern Development Bank Notes, which were part of a single currency planned for the Japanese "Greater East Asia Co-Prosperity Sphere" to bring occupied countries under a single currency. When the Allied forces were on the verge of retaking Yangon at the end of April 1945, Japanese bank staff similarly – though unsuccessfully – tried to burn all their banknotes before fleeing the city. Glenn S. Hensley, an

American soldier who arrived in Yangon with the first Allied troops, found the streets around this building littered with banknotes, "thick as fallen leaves".

Since the war, most critical changes in Myanmar's fiscal policy were administered through this building. In the lead-up to Independence, the bank was renamed the Union Bank of Burma and, in March 1952, severed ties with the pound sterling leading to the establishment of a distinct Burmese currency. The first *kyat* and *pya* (1 *kyat* = 100 *pya*) were issued here on 1 July 1952.

Later, during the socialist era, the Union Bank of Burma oversaw the controversial demonetization of the *kyat* in 1964. On 17 May 1964, it was announced that 50-*kyat* and 100-*kyat* notes would no longer be considered legal tender and that compensation of up to 500 *kyat* per person would be provided to those who returned their banknotes to the bank within one week.

Over the past decades, the bank has changed its name and structure in accordance with changing government policies. In 1970, when all banks were merged into a single bank called the People's Bank of the Union of Burma, this building was its head office. In 1975, four state-owned banks were established: the Union of Burma Bank (in this building), the Myanmar Economic Bank, the Myanmar Foreign Trade Bank, and the Myanmar Agriculture Bank. In 1990, following banking reforms that took place after the political upheavals of 1988, the bank was renamed the Central Bank of Myanmar and became sole issuer of currency and banker to the government.

PRESENT

Since 1993, this building has been the head office of the private Myawaddy Bank, owned by the Union of Myanmar Economic Holdings Limited (UMEHL). Not only is this building historic for having been at the centre of changes in fiscal policy throughout most of the past century, but it is also of considerable architectural significance. Dr. Kyaw Lat, Honorary Professor at Yangon Technological University's Department of Architecture, considers the Myawaddy Bank his favourite colonial-era building. "Most buildings in downtown Yangon come under the banner of 'eclecticism', which is a period of architecture that mixed together various different and mismatched styles," he says. "The Myawaddy Bank is a more classical building, inspired by Palladianism and neo-Classicism. It is purpose-built and supremely suited to its purpose – the pillars emulate the façade of a Greek temple and are designed to indicate honesty, stability, and straightforwardness, which are the qualities people desire in a banking service."

USELESS CASH

Streets near the Bank of India building were literally covered with paper money. As thick as fallen leaves, the useless currency lay abandoned just as was the city after the occupying Japanese forces fled during World War II. Frank Bond, 1945.

WAR DAMAGE

Burned-out Bank of Indian Yangon's central business district. British 14th Army troops are rolling into town after its abandonment by the Japanese during World War II. In this shot, the Jeep carries three Indian troopers and a map-reading "Britisher". Glenn S. Hensley, 1945.

10 MYANMAR OIL & GAS ENTERPRISE

formerly
BURMAH OIL COMPANY

Location: 604-608 Merchant Road

Built: 1908

Architect/Contractor: Robinson & Mundy (contractor)

Originally built as the headquarters of a Scottish trading firm, this building later became the office of one of colonial Britain's most profitable enterprises.

PAST

This building was designed as an office for the Glaswegian firm Finlay, Fleming & Company, one of the top mercantile houses operating in Myanmar in the early part of the 20th century. The company exported cotton and fabric dyes, and imported a broad variety of merchandise from Europe, such as milk, shoes, paint, Melrose gin, and Grant's whisky from Scotland. Finlay, Fleming & Co. also acted as the managing agent of another Glaswegian company, the Burmah Oil Company (BOC), which later took over this building.

As the Rangoon headquarters of the BOC, the building was known as Yenan House (*yenan* means oil in Burmese). The company was founded in 1886 to work the oil fields in what was then known as Upper Burma; after the third Anglo-Burmese war ended with the fall of the royal dynasty, the British Crown leased extensive tracts to the BOC.

In the days before widespread electricity, the BOC was associated with keeping Yangon alight, as the company's main products in its early years were candles and kerosene lamps. Indeed, the company's oil products lit homes and fuelled vehicles across the world, from Aden to Shanghai and Tokyo.

The BOC enjoyed its most profitable years during the 1920s when it was listed among the top 10 manufacturing firms of Great Britain. At that time, the company had 100 employees in England and over 40,000 in India, Myanmar, and Iran [then Persia]. By the 1930s, Myanmar's total crude oil production had risen to over one million tons annually, with 80 percent of this amount being produced by the BOC.

As the company made a sizeable profit from Burmese natural resources it became an obvious target for the nationalist movement and an antagonistic symbol of colonial rapaciousness. In the early 1920s, when Burmese nationalists launched a boycott of foreign goods, people were encouraged to stop buying BOC candles to light Buddhist shrines. When oil workers went on strike for better working conditions in the late 1930s, this building became a focal point for protestors. The strikes linked up with demonstrations led by university students and became a key event in Myanmar's struggle for independence from British rule.

One day, in 1939, oil workers managed to block all entrances to the BOC's head office by lying down on the pavements around this building. When protestors had not dispersed by the end of office hours, British staff became concerned about the female employees within the building, most of whom were Anglo-Burmese. They created a human bridge across the prostrate crowd, handing the women from man to man until they were clear of the protestors. The local press made much of this curious event the following day, running headlines like, "British Officers Abusing Local Girls!"

When World War II broke out, the BOC found itself in control of one of the key resources needed to fight a war, namely petrol. Once it became clear that Myanmar would fall to the Japanese, the BOC had to join the so-called "scorched earth" campaign operated by the British government, which sought to destroy anything that might be used by the Japanese when they took over the country. In March 1942, with the Japanese closing in on Yangon, the BOC was among the last of the British companies to leave the city. One of its managers remained in the Drawing Office of this building shredding and burning maps, plans, and other potentially useful paperwork. Beyond Yangon, BOC staff systematically destroyed the company's oil refineries, wells, pumping equipment, drilling machinery, tools, and power supplies.

opposite:
Under scaffolding, the Myanmar Oil & Gas Enterprise is one of five buildings which underwent basic renovation [see page 39]

When BOC employees returned to the office after the war, they were amazed to find that many buildings along Merchant Road had survived the heavy bombing. Their building was still standing but the interior of the office was "a shambles with no furniture or equipment". A history of the company notes, "The files had all been destroyed or removed before evacuation, and the control of production and refining and resumption of marketing needed to be organised virtually from scratch."

Starting from scratch led to downsizing and, in the years after independence, the BOC shared this building with the Ideal Nursing Home, also known as the San Pya Clinic.

In 1963, the BOC was sold to the Burmese government. The process is recorded in the company annals as being unusual when compared to other handovers during the nationalization process under the new Revolutionary Council, as negotiations were smooth and mutually agreeable. Afterwards, however, BOC British staff had difficulties leaving the country as their bank balances, pension contributions, and baggage were held up for "unconscionably long periods".

This building became the headquarters of the state-owned Myanmar Oil & Gas Enterprise, which stayed here until the government's move to Nay Pyi Taw in 2005. Through a series of mergers and acquisitions the BOC later became the oil and gas giant BP (British Petroleum).

Advertisement from 1954 showing the Myanmar Oil & Gas Enterprise building

PRESENT

This building is currently empty and was one of five chosen for renovation by the Ministry of Construction (see Saving Yangon's Heritage, page 39). During Cyclone Nargis in 2008, most of the roofing was destroyed and the renovation effort replaced the roof slabs to protect the building until further repairs can be made. When it was first constructed, this building was one of the most imposing buildings on Merchant Road – today it stands dwarfed by two modern tower blocks.

11 MERCHANT ROAD BANKS

Location:
These banks are on Merchant Road, between Sule Pagoda Road and Shwebontha Street

At 550-2 Merchant Road is the Innwa Bank, which was privately renovated in 2011. The building was originally the premises of Oppenheimer & Company, a firm of general merchants that began doing business in Yangon in 1885. The company dabbled in various trades; supplying uniforms for the British police force in Burma and the Malay States, producing gear for working elephants, and also importing Underwood typewriters, Whitfield's safes, and Singer cycles, among many other popular brand-name items of the time. The building has been beautifully restored by its current tenant, the Innwa Bank. The former Innwa Bank office, located next door at 554-6 Merchant Road in the former Mercantile Bank of India building, was moved into this renovated property and plans are in place to renovate the neighbouring property as well.

Such corporate involvement in renovating old properties may encourage other companies to locate their offices in old buildings (other examples include the *Myanmar Times* office on Bo Aung Kyaw Street). Corporations could also sponsor restoration work, thereby generating publicity through their investment in the city's heritage.

opposite:
Building details, former Mercantile Bank of India

Along Merchant Road to the west stands the former Hong Kong Shanghai Banking Corporation [HSBC] building. The HSBC was nationalised on 23 February 1963 along with all 31 private banks in Myanmar [14 foreign and 17 national] and became the People's Bank No. 9. Today, the building is used by the Myanmar Foreign Trade Bank.

Further west, at 625 Merchant Road, is the former Netherlands Trading Society building, now the First Private Bank. At 666 Merchant Road, on the corner of Shwebontha Street, is the former Punjab National Bank. The Merchant Road side of this building is currently owned by the Myanmar Livestock & Fisheries Development Bank, while the Shwebontha Street side houses a number of small offices. Next to the Shwebontha Street entrance is a marble wall plaque for The Life Insurance Corporation of India, Rangoon branch – one of the few remaining signs with the anglicised name for Yangon, "Rangoon" [see also the back gates of City Hall, page 42]. The area beneath the portico on this side of the former bank is used as a pavement teashop where the so-called "stock merchants" of Shwebontha Street gather in the afternoons to play chess and checkers after a day's trading.

A VANISHED BUILDING
The State Commercial Bank was located next to the Hong Kong Shanghai Banking Corporation on Mahabandoola Garden Street. Before it became a bank, this building was home to the Silver Grill, a famous Yangon eatery owned by the Armenian proprietor who later took over the Strand Hotel [20]. This image was painted by the British manager of the State Commercial Bank, Mr. G. M. Godley. The painting hung in his office until the bank was nationalised and was later salvaged from a pile of rubbish before the building was demolished.

RANGOON COSMOPOLITAN

Su Lin Lewis

In one sense, Rangoon (now Yangon) was always cosmopolitan, even when ruled by a Burmese king. For over a thousand years, Dagon, as it was then known, drew Buddhists from all over the region as the site of the Shwedagon pagoda. In the sixteenth century, via the nearby port-city of Pegu (Bago), the town was connected by trading routes to a region at the centre of the global spice trade. King Alaungpaya renamed the town Yangon and made it the chief seaport of the Irawaddy Delta in 1755, leaving Portuguese and Armenian traders to run the city. It soon became a centre for Indian, Chinese, as well as European traders, then seen as 'undesirables' who had defected by the East India Company and married local women.

When occupying British armies destroyed the city in 1852, they remade it on a mathematical grid resembling lower Manhattan, structured around its waterfront. The encouragement of free trade and the building of new, modern infrastructure drew thousands of immigrants from all over the world. Traders as well as revolutionaries, religious pundits, musicians, circus-performers, and cinema magnates arrived from all over Asia.

In the 1920s, a golden age of travel, Rangoon was a key stopover point on the steamship route from India to China. One could cruise to Singapore in two days, to Calcutta in four, to Shanghai in six. A slew of international writers began to put Rangoon on the global literary map, from Rudyard Kipling and Somerset Maugham to Aldous Huxley, H.G. Wells, and Pablo Neruda (see page 35). Some came for love, like the English surrealist writer Anna Kavan, who followed her husband, an Indian Civil Service officer, to Rangoon in 1920. She left him two years later, though she set one of her finest novels, *Who am I?*, in a hazy Burmese landscape.

In colonial memoirs, Rangoon was often referred to as an 'alien city', more welcoming to foreigners than the Burmese. In 1940, just before Japanese bombs fell from the sky, W. G. Grant, the English editor of the *Rangoon Times* noted of Rangoon:

> She houses Indians in thousands, and there Europeans build bungalows, run commercial concerns, and smoke in clubs. She has a Chinese quarter where you can pray to Sun Yat Sen or merely have your milk pail repaired. Along her mathematically precise streets walk Japanese, Greeks, Armenians, Jews, Australians, Americans, Spaniards from Brazil and Malays from Singapore. Rangoon opens her arms to the world. She is the soul of hospitality, the ideal hostess. And yet with a heart for all men she has a heart of her own.... Her cosmopolitanism has made her subtle.... Perhaps when all is said and done she does love Burma. It is her home in a physical sense. But she does not live in Burmese life. She lives a thousand lives, and dodging here and there amongst them, is an elusive ghost that smiles like Burma...

And yet, it was Rangoon's place as a nexus of global trade and communication technology that put a young generation of Burmese in touch with the wider world. Inspired by books and periodicals, gramophones and cinema, and their interactions with visitors to the city, they wrote novels, they made music and films, and they pushed for political change. Rangoon was cosmopolitan in its diversity, but it was also where Burmese came to feel, and become, 'modern'. As a city near the sea, Rangoon is destined, like so many cities, to look both outward and in, to welcome foreigners and resist foreign domination, to house millions of different lives, and tell an infinite number of stories.

Su Lin Lewis *finished her PhD in History at Cambridge University in 2010 and is currently working on a book on cosmopolitan Asia.*

D PANSODAN STREET, LOWER BLOCK

During British times, lower Pansodan Street [then called Phayre Street] was considered the best business address in town. The street was lined with major banks, department stores, and the offices of the rich and influential among the merchant community. In the lowest block, between Merchant Road and Strand Road, all but one of the buildings date back to the first half of the 20th century and the block offers a rare vista of heritage structures that conjure up the city's cosmopolitan past.

On the corner of Pansodan Street and Merchant Road is the **Internal Revenue Department [12]**, a former office building built by Surti Indian merchants. Opposite is the **Lokanat Gallery Building [13]**, the once glamorous Sofaer's Buildings commissioned by a Baghdadi Jewish trader and filled with high-end shops and offices. Down towards the river is the **Inland Waterways Department [14]**, originally the grand offices of the Irrawaddy Flotilla Company, and the equally splendid building that once housed Grindlays Bank and is now the **Myanmar Agricultural Development Bank [15]**. On the other side of Pansodan stand **Myanmar Economic Bank 1 [16]** and **Myanmar Economic Bank 2 [17]**, which were originally the British banks Lloyds and Chartered, respectively. At the bottom of the lower block, on the corner of Strand Road, are the Port Authority [21] and the Yangon Division Court [22], both described in Section E.

Pansodan Street was once lined with rain trees that were cut down after plans were laid to widen the road in the late 1980s. During the process some of the porticos of the old buildings were demolished to make space for road traffic. The two that remain – now incongruously extending over the road – are on the east side of Pansodan Street on the Inland Waterways Department and the Myanmar Agricultural Development Bank buildings. In the late afternoon, the west side of the street falls into shade and makeshift teashops set up stools and low tables along the pavement to cater to customers at the end of the workday.

This neighbourhood also has literary and artistic associations. Since the 1950s, it has been the setting for the popular Pansodan book market, which used to spread out along the pavements and beneath the porticos of the middle block of Pansodan Street. Affectionately dubbed the "street-side university", the market attracted an intellectual clientele and book browsers were likely to bump into famous poets, novelists, and historians searching for books both old and new. In the early 2000s, a fire destroyed one of the main buildings sheltering the market and many book vendors moved to 37th Street, just behind Pansodan Street, where a number of small bookshops are located.

There is no debating the supreme architectural value of this single city block. Pansodan Street leads into Strand Road, which runs along the river and offers a similarly dense stretch of heritage buildings [see Section E].

12 INTERNAL REVENUE DEPARTMENT

formerly
RANDER HOUSE

Location: west side of Pansodan Street, corner of Merchant Road

Built: 1932

Architect/ Contractor: Unknown

This simple but striking five-storey building bears a likeness to the American Classical style of 1920s downtown Chicago, with a few finely restrained art deco flourishes.

PAST

The name "Rander House" inscribed on the façade indicates that this building was commissioned by Surti Indian traders who came from Rander, a port town in Gujurat, India. The Surti Indians, who get their name from the city of Surat (also in Gujarat), first came to Myanmar under the reign of King Mindon (r. 1853-1878) and many moved to Yangon to pursue business opportunities in the wake of the British conquest. Indians from Rander considered themselves distinct from the main group of Surti Indians and are first recorded in the city as early as 1854 when a Rander native called Moola Hashim erected a bamboo mosque. The mosque, later constructed as a masonry building, still stands today on Shwebontha Street, and is known as the Surtee Sunni Jumma Masjid.

It is believed that the family who commissioned this building left Myanmar during or shortly after World War II, along with hundreds of thousands of other Indians. Today, the town of Rander in India still has Burmese influences that were carried home with those returning traders; their cuisine features Burmese specialties like "Rangooni *paratha*" (crispy fried flatbread stuffed with mutton or chicken) and *ohn-noke khaukswe* (coconut chicken noodle soup).

After Independence, the embassy of the Islamic Republic of Pakistan was located in Rander House while the embassy of the Republic of India was situated in Randeria House, directly across the road.

In the 1950s, the British Council library was set up in this building and hosted a number of local clubs such as the Burma Photographic Society and the Burma Stamp Club. Other offices in the building at that time included an outlet of Mitsubishi machinery and the Yangon office of Dawson's Bank (which had its main offices in the Ayeyarwaddy Delta and provided loans to farmers), as well as some government accounting offices. Later, during the socialist period, the British Council library was shut down and moved to the British Embassy (19).

PRESENT

The upper floors of Rander House are maintained as residential flats and the lower floors are currently being used as offices for the Internal Revenue Department.

Next to Rander House, on Merchant Road, is the current-day Indian Embassy (545-547 Merchant Street). The building, built in 1914, still displays the faded sign of its previous use as the "Oriental Assurance Building".

PEDESTRIANISING PANSODAN

As the lower block of Pansodan Street does not channel much traffic flow through the city, Burmese architects and urban planners hope that it can be pedestrianised and turned into a unique attraction for tourists and residents alike. One architect envisions a dramatic night market with the heritage buildings lit up in the background, while another suggests a special jetty that would allow visitors to alight on the riverbank and stroll up Pansodan Street, much as visitors might have done a century ago.

On behalf of a group of concerned architects, Statement Architecture & Design firm created a model of this block with suggestions for the potential development of each building which included restaurants, an art gallery, hotel, department store, and multi-storey parking lot. The model aims to preserve as much as possible of the area's architecture and ambiance while improving the physical environment with walkways and landscaping, and providing guidelines for the private sector to become actively engaged in the conservation process.

13 LOKANAT GALLERY BUILDING

formerly
SOFAER'S BUILDINGS

Location: 58-62 Pansodan Street

Built: circa 1906

Architect/ Contractor: Thomas Swales

With its Italianate flourishes, this stately building was once one of the city's most prestigious business addresses. Built by a Baghdadi Jewish trader whose passion was architecture, it remains a tantalising symbol of Yangon's cosmopolitan past.

PAST

Here, Yangon residents once purchased Theodoro Vafiadis Egyptian cigarettes, Lighthouse Munich Beer, and candies imported from England. Though the building also housed legal and financial offices such as the China Mutual Life Insurance Company, it was best known for its purveyors of fine liqueurs and commodities.

Also located in this building was the Reuters Telegram Company, Ltd., which fed news to Burma in the early years of the 20th century. Another tenant was Philip Klier, a German photographer who came to Myanmar in 1877. Klier ran a shop selling Burmese souvenirs and pictorial postcards; today his photographs remain one of the primary windows onto old Myanmar.

Building details, former Sofaer's Buildings

Other tenants of the building who illustrate the cosmopolitanism of Yangon at that time include Mr. J. D. Pappademitriou, a Greek leather merchant, and Mr. M. D'Cruz, a Filipino hairdresser who first came to the city with Harmston's Circus, a travelling menagerie of performing wild animals.

Originally known as Sofaer's Buildings, this complex was designed by Isaac A. Sofaer, a Jewish trader born in Baghdad in 1867. Brought to Myanmar as a young boy by his parents, Sofaer was educated at St. Paul's School (3). He and his brother, Meyer Sofaer, set up a successful business importing wine, liquor, and specialty foods. Isaac was a prominent member of Rangoon society, a trustee at the Synagogue (which still stands at 85, 26th Street) and a member of the Municipal Council.

Sofaer descendants recall Meyer as the business-minded brother and Isaac as the dreamer; while Isaac sat on a stool in front of construction sites watching the buildings he commissioned materialise, Meyer worked hard to build up the family business by importing delicacies from around the world [the variety of products he sourced included sardines from Norway, olives from Spain, and whisky from the British Isles].

The brothers were part of a Jewish community that numbered around 2,100 in its heyday in the early decades of the 20th century. The community was comprised mostly of traders from the Middle East who followed trade routes carved out by the East India Company and the British Empire, which eventually led them to Myanmar. Most left the country after World War II or nationalization in the early 1960s, and only a handful remain in Yangon today. The Sofaers left much earlier. At some point before 1917, they faced severe financial difficulties and, when the banks foreclosed on their business loans, they lost this building along with all their other properties. By the time Isaac Sofaer passed away in Rangoon in 1926, most members of his family had moved to India. Isaac's son, Abraham, had left after World War I to try his luck on the London stage; he later moved on to Hollywood where his most prominent appearances included a dual role as the judge and surgeon in the 1946 Powell & Pressburger film production, *A Matter of Life and Death*, and a guest appearance in the first season of the cult television series *Star Trek*. The rest of the Sofaer family settled mostly in the UK and in California, USA. Long after the Sofaers relinquished their claim on the building, it still bore the family name and was listed as "Sofaer's Buildings" well into the 1920s.

It is thought that the family of Indian Surti traders who owned Rander House across the road purchased this building, as its name changed in the 1930s to "Randeria Buildings" or "Randeria House". After World War II this building was transferred into government hands. The Forestry Department was located on the top floor and the Sugar Project Board, which oversaw sugar factories under the Directorate of Industries, was based here. During the socialist period, the Ministry of Industry No. 1 operated a government store on the ground floor that doled out rations of rice, cooking oil, and sugar at subsidised rates.

In 1971, the Lokanat Gallery was established on the first floor and became one of the few early venues for showcasing contemporary art in Myanmar. The gallery was supported by U Ba Than, a retired military man and art lover, and counted among its founding members a variety of artists such as the traditionalist painter Hla Shein [a Finance Ministry official in the 1950s], Kin Maung "Bank" [considered the father of modernist painting in Burma], and the famous vagabond painter Paw Oo Thet. Named after the guardian spirit of the universe in Myanmar legend, the Lokanat Gallery has as its motto "truth, beauty, love" and the gallery requires that its members do not paint with the sole aim of gaining fame, profit, or power.

PRESENT

As with Rander House across the road, this building is now partially occupied by the Internal Revenue Department. The Ministry of Industry No. 1's government store is still located on the ground floor, selling an array of "Made in Myanmar" products. Other parts of the building have been leased out to a variety of businesses; photocopy shops, the Myanmar Overseas Seafarers Association, teashops, a law firm, and a small guesthouse.

In some parts of the ground floor and the Lokanat Gallery, the original tiles, specially imported from Manchester by Isaac Sofaer over a hundred years ago, are still in place. Parts of the interior are severely deteriorated; the upper floors are semi-derelict, the courtyard has become a rubbish dump, as has the lift shaft, and the teakwood staircases leading to the top floor are rotting away.

Paw Oo Thet

Born in Mandalay, the great Burmese artist Paw Oo Thet (1936-1993) learned to paint as a young boy. During World War II, he lost his right hand while playing with a grenade and had to relearn how to paint with his left hand. He later drew cartoons for newspapers but became most well-known for distinctive paintings that blended traditional Myanmar topics and Western techniques. Paw Oo Thet was given a small room at the Lokanat Gallery and lived here until the final years of his life.

Self-portrait in Robe, 1967. Oil on canvas. Collection of Paw Oo Thet Family, Mandalay.

CHILDHOOD MEMORIES

Isaac Sofaer's youngest son, Ellis, was born in 1904. In his unpublished memoir Gaya, His Childhood, *he recalls his father's pride in the building:*

"My father was spurred by ambition to try his fortune in speculative building. He had a splendid office block erected, which he named Sofaer's Buildings. My father's gamble cost him dearly. This building was instrumental in deflecting sharply the course of our lives, but at the time it was full of future promise. My father's pride in it was obvious. He took my mother and all the family to see it when it was nearing completion, and I remember running around on its roof, chasing a golf ball that my sister Esther had acquired from somewhere..."

POTENTIAL

This building is of particular concern to members of the Association of Myanmar Architects who believe that restoration work must begin soon if it is to be saved.

There are communities surrounding this building that could potentially be better accommodated inside it. The back of the building opens onto 37th Street where vendors cater to the lunchtime crowd of office workers. One local resident suggested the creation of a food hall along the Singaporean model so that vendors can sell their wares in a sanitary and orderly way. Another neighbourhood resident raised the possibility of relocating the Pansodan book market and book dealers into a floor of this building.

14 INLAND WATERWAYS DEPARTMENT

formerly
IRRAWADDY FLOTILLA COMPANY

Location:
50 Pansodan Street

Built: 1933

Architect/ Contractor:
A. G. Bray (architect), Arthur Flavell & Co. (contractor)

This gracefully proportioned white building with its colonnaded façade was built as the headquarters of the legendary Irrawaddy Flotilla Company.

PAST

The Irrawaddy Flotilla Company was set up in Myanmar in 1865 by Todd, Findlay & Co. and had its head offices in Glasgow. From a humble beginning with just four steamers and three barges plying the Ayeyarwaddy (formerly Irrawaddy) River the company grew rapidly and, by the 1920s, its advertising claimed that it ran "The Largest Fleet of Inland Steamers Operating in the World". The company's vessels provided river transport throughout Burma, delivering passengers, mail, and freight. By the eve of World War II, it operated 600 vessels, shifting eight million passengers and a quarter million tons of cargo per year.

The original office was at 4 Phayre (now Pansodan) Street, where the Port Authority (21) now stands. This office, constructed during the company's heyday in the 1930s, is a steel-framed, brick-built building that was designed with a tropical setting in mind; all its entrances and windows are recessed so that no direct sunlight enters the building and heats up the interior.

In 1927, the General Manager of the Irrawaddy Flotilla Company built himself a home just north of the downtown area. He called the house Belmont and followed it with additional homes called Belwood and Belstone, as well as a chummery for bachelors.

Building details, former Irrawaddy Flotilla Company

above and opposite: Architectural drawing of the Irrawaddy Flotilla Company building, 1931, the building under construction, 1932, and exterior and interior views on completion, 1933

Belmont is today the residence of the British ambassador and senior embassy employees are accommodated in the residential compound. Additionally, four flats were built on the top floor of the Irrawaddy Flotilla's office, as staff housing in the city centre.

During World War II, the Irrawaddy Flotilla fleet was requisitioned by the British Governor to transport ammunition and evacuate supplies and people. This building was evacuated at the 11th hour and employees were ordered to sink all unused flotillas. The remainder of the fleet was sunk at Mandalay. The company manager at the time, John Morton, wrote in his diary of 28 April 1942, "We are being chased out quicker now than was expected and I have orders for more sinkings here at Kyaukmyaung [about 45 miles north of Mandalay]. There are over two hundred of our fleet sunk at Mandalay. Imagine how I felt drilling holes in their bottoms with a Bren gun."

On 1 June 1948, shortly after Independence, the Burmese government took over the company and its much-denuded assets. As a state enterprise, this building became known as the Inland Water Transport Board.

PRESENT

Though river transport has been superceded by road, rail, and air, this building still houses the same office, now called the Inland Waterways Department. At the entrances for No. 44 and No. 54 Pansodan Street the words "Irrawaddy Chambers" remain carved above the archways.

15 MYANMAR AGRICULTURAL DEVELOPMENT BANK

formerly
GRINDLAYS BANK

Location: 26/42 Pansodan Street

Built: circa 1930

Architect/ Contractor: Unknown

This eye-catching white building boasts some unique features, such as a curved art deco portico above the entranceway and gargoyles in the form of roaring lions along the roof.

PAST

This building originally housed the Yangon branch of Grindlays Bank, which was then one of the largest overseas banks operating in India and had been established there since 1854. Grindlays changed hands a number of times; in 1924 it was purchased by the National Provincial Bank and then in 1958 merged with the National Bank of India, which maintained a branch in this building throughout the 1950s along with the offices of various accountants and auditors. (Much later, in 2000, Grindlays was bought by the Standard Chartered group.)

In a company history, one British staff member recalled the different era of banking that existed in the 1920s: "It was the Bank's proud boast that all customers were known personally to the partners and staff and the Bank was known affectionately as 'Father Grindlay' to whom all worries could be taken." In February 1970, this property was repurposed as Myanmar's National

Museum [previously located in the now demolished Jubilee Hall]. It was a challenge turning a bank into a museum, as the 1979 edition of the *Lonely Planet Burma: a Travel Survival Kit* noted: "At one time you had to leave the ground floor, go out on to the street and re-enter the museum next door! There is now access from the ground floor, but it is very easy to miss. The only sign for the upstairs is in Burmese and you have to first of all make your way through an empty room, round the lift shaft and up some dingy stairs!" After the museum was moved to specially constructed premises on Pyay Road in 1996, this building returned to its banking past and became a branch office of the Myanmar Industrial Development Bank and the Myanmar Agricultural Development Bank.

PRESENT

Today, the Myanmar Agricultural Development Bank maintains a branch office on the first floor while the ground floor is empty and unused.

Next door [22-24 Pansodan Street] is a smaller building owned by the Ministry of Information. After Independence, it was used as an information department for the government public relations and press liaison office, and as a reading room. It is now leased out to different tenants but the Ministry still runs a small library on the ground floor.

Building details, Grindlay Bank; and *The Journey of the Lion Throne* [Page 93, overleaf]

16 MYANMAR ECONOMIC BANK 1

formerly
LLOYDS BANK

Location: 43/45 Pansodan

Built: circa 1921

Architect/ Contractor: Unknown

This three-storey building survives as a classic example of a mid-sized office in downtown Yangon that would not have looked out of place on the streets of London.

PAST

The British bank Lloyds took over this building in 1923 after purchasing Cox & Company, an army agency set up to serve British garrisons stationed in Egypt, India, and Myanmar. By 1941, Lloyds was operating two branches in Myanmar.

After being forced to evacuate during World War II, Lloyds operated as a "bank in exile" in Lahore and planned its return along with other foreign banks under the cheeky mission name "Operation Shylock" – Shylock is the unscrupulous moneylender in William Shakespeare's *Merchant of Venice*. Lloyds staff managed to return to this Yangon office in December 1945, just a few months after the end of the war.

THE JOURNEY OF THE LION THRONE

When this building housed the National Museum, it had one very memorable exhibit – the Lion Throne of the last king of Myanmar. The throne was 26 feet high and, having been manoeuvered into the old bank building with some difficulty, dominated the front room.

The throne had already been on an epic journey. Originally located in the royal palace of Mandalay, it was looted by the British after the third Anglo-Burmese War in 1886, along with the royal regalia, and placed in a museum in Calcutta [now Kolkata], India. After Burma's independence, Lord Mountbatten, who was then India's Governor-General, returned the throne to Yangon. It was transported from India in 60 cases containing 450 pieces that had to be reassembled on arrival.

Hubert C. Gotts, the manager of Lloyds in Yangon, was one of the first returnees and was shocked by the large-scale looting that had taken place. All the bank's furniture had disappeared. The banking hall was utterly empty, but for a short length of battered counter with broken railings. The floor was inches deep with ash and filth. Gotts immediately set up cleaning the building. One of his priorities was to repair the strong room, which had been dynamited by the Japanese army; luckily, the security company Chubb had a representative touring war-damaged cities in the region and the vault was quickly fixed. In just under a month, on 23 January 1946, the bank was able to open its doors for business. Gotts later wrote, "We were soon helping to finance the rice crop and so get exports going again to earn the foreign currency the country so badly needed."

A few months after Myanmar's Independence from Britain in 1948, Gotts was involved in a spat with the newly independent government of the Union of Burma. Gotts had written to the Ministry of Foreign Affairs at Prome Court [29] requesting approval for the four-year appointment of a new assistant from England after one of his senior Indian assistants left. The Ministry granted permission on the condition that Lloyds train a Burmese citizen to replace the British appointee within the four-year time period of his posting. Lloyds demurred and Gotts wrote back to the Ministry arguing that no other country restricted recruitment of foreign staff by authorised banks: "While we sympathise with the Un on Government's Burmanisation Policy, you will appreciate that we cannot agree to be bound by any rigid condition governing staff recruitment."

The government's "Burmanisation" policy expected businesses to train Burmese citizens in their employ to assume charge of more high-ranking posts and thereby progressively reduce the need for the immigration of non-Burmese. Gotts, however, concluded that, "Unless the Bank can have a reasonably free hand over staff recruitment and postings, we shall have very seriously to consider the whole question of the Bank's future in Burma." Not long after that, Lloyds closed its Myanmar branches.

PRESENT

The building is currently in use as the state-owned Myanmar Economic Bank 1. Next door is the only non-colonial-era building on the lower Pansodan block, the Myanmar Economic Savings Bank 1.

Lloyds Bank, circa 1950s

17 MYANMAR ECONOMIC BANK 2

formerly
CHARTERED BANK

Location:
27 Pansodan Street

Built: 1939-1941

Architect/ Contractor:
G. Douglas Smart, Palmer & Turner (architect)
Arthur Flavell & Co. (contractor)

With its pagoda-inspired entrance tower, this art deco building lined with cut stone tiles occupies a proud location on Pansodan Street and is still often referred to as the "Chartered Bank" building.

PAST

This building was designed for the Chartered Bank of India, Australia and China, one of the leading British exchange banks of its time, with headquarters in Bishopsgate, London. A 1920s advertisement for the bank boasted that it had branches across the world, from Amritsar (India) to Zamboanga (the Philippines). The Chartered Bank is still a big name in global financing, known today as the Standard Chartered Bank.

The bank opened its Rangoon branch in 1858 at a time when business was booming in the colonies. In *Realms of Silver*, the Scottish author Sir Compton MacKenzie wrote of that period, "There were not many places in the world, even during the boom of the early sixties, that could afford to pay equally high charges for banking facilities, and the prosperity of Rangoon can be realised when a building site bought by the Bank in August 1864 for 20,000 rupees could have been sold at a profit of a least 50 per cent within less than a couple of years."

above:
Building details, Chartered Bank

below, right:
Architectural drawings for Chartered Bank building by Palmer & Turner

The bank moved from an early office on Phayre (now Pansodan) Street to Strand Road but by the late 1880s was in dire need of better accommodation, as the dilapidated building it operated from was said to be "disgraceful" both inside and out. The bank purchased a plot of land on the present site but then had to wait some 10 years before constructing a new office as labour and building materials were considered too costly at the time. The building that stands today replaces an earlier one constructed in the late 1890s by the architect Henry Hoyne-Fox.

The architect of this current building, G. Douglas Smart, was a partner of the architectural firm Palmer & Turner, and ran the firm's office in Yangon, closing it down when World War II broke out. Palmer & Turner was set up in 1868 during a period of frenetic development in Hong Kong. In the early decades of the 20th century, the firm expanded to India, Malaysia, and China, where it was responsible for many of the buildings still standing on the Shanghai Bund. Today, the firm is known as the P&T Group and is the oldest and largest international architectural engineering practice in Southeast Asia.

365 LOST KEYS

When the Chartered Bank building was surveyed for damage after World War II, it was found that most of the keys were missing. The building had a total of 365 locks, which included keys to the records room, side entrances, and caretaker's accommodation, as well as keys to the French windows in the tiffin room, stationery and pantry cupboards, and various lavatories. An entire new set of door handles, locks, and keys had to be ordered from the original supplier, Messrs. James Gibbons, one of the UK's most reputable locksmiths.

This building was officially completed in January 1941 and was, by all accounts, a dazzlingly modern structure. With a total floor space of over 32,280 square feet, the building boasted a spacious banking hall lit by high windows and a skylight as well as a basement with state-of-the-art vaults and the city's first underground parking lot. The steel-frame building was constructed with reinforced concrete. The floors were overlaid with Terrazzo tiles and the interior was plastered with Victorite. The roof was protected with three layers of Mastic sealant intercepted by waterproof fabric and a final layer of shingle.

Just a year after it its completion, however, the bank had to abandon the building when the Japanese army marched on Yangon in World War II. By January 1942 well-prepared bank staff had duplicated records and requested permission to ship them along with the bank's securities to Calcutta [now Kolkata]. A month later, the bank loaded its staff, cash, and bullion onto a train specially requisitioned for the evacuation of the city's banks to Mandalay. Senior staff carried the remaining records to Calcutta by air. When the Japanese arrived, this building was occupied by the Japanese commercial bank Yokohama Specie Bank.

Having sat out the war in a temporary office in Lahore, India, the Chartered Bank's managerial staff were incredulous to find the building intact when they returned to Yangon at the end of 1945. The architect, G. Douglas Smart, had also returned to the city after the war and surveyed the premises to list necessary repairs. Smart found no structural damage to the building's masonry, columns, or floors and the façade remained miraculously untouched by shrapnel, bombs, or blast marks. As with other properties, the interior had been thoroughly looted; steel doors, window frames, electrical fittings, and ceiling fans had been stolen. Even the bronze lettering on the front parapet of the portico had been removed.

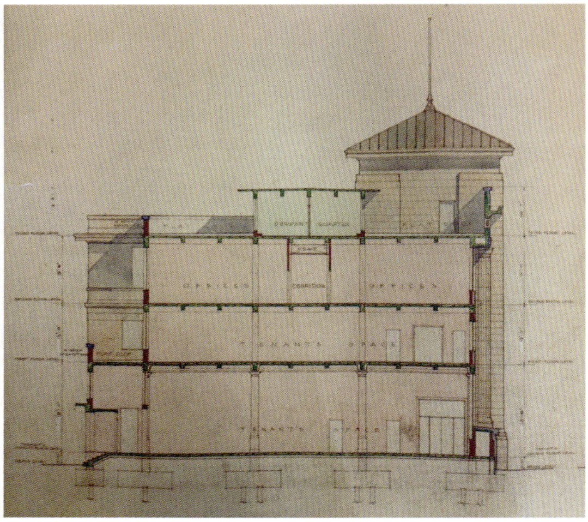

Architectural drawings for Chartered Bank building by Palmer & Turner

Chartered Bank continued to operate in Myanmar after the country's Independence from Britain. As it had done before the war, the bank leased office space in the back of the building to various tenants. After Independence, these included the Burma Chamber of Commerce, the United States Information Services Library run by the US Embassy, and the Great Eastern Life Assurance company managed by Balthazar & Sons.

Various repairs and refurbishments were carried out to both the building's exterior and interior over the following years. In 1954, after an exceptionally warm hot season, air-conditioning units were installed in the manager's office. In 1957, the pre-war electrical system was condemned by government inspectors and the entire building had to be rewired. The Chartered Bank's last interior renovation took place in 1960.

On 23 February 1963, Chartered Bank was nationalised along with all other commercial banks in Myanmar and became People's Bank No. 2.

PRESENT

The building currently houses the state-owned Myanmar Economic Bank 2. Though the building is somewhat rundown, some original features have survived, such as the splendid entrance doors on the corner of Pansodan and Bank Street. In March 2012 the building was repainted in shades of blue.

CONSTRUCTING YANGON'S COLONIAL CORE

The key administrative and commercial buildings that make up Yangon's "colonial core" are today a legacy set in stone, but their construction was fraught with logistical challenges, differences of opinion, and the unfinished search for an appropriate colonial aesthetic.

When British government officials began designing the new capital of "Rangoon", they made use of military engineers such as Lieutenant Alexander Fraser who drew up the plan for the city. In the 1860s, this Royal Engineer corps was merged with the government's Public Works Department, which had been established in India. The newly amalgamated department was responsible for all state construction, from roads and bridges to hospitals, courthouses, schools, post offices, and village halls.

The early buildings in Myanmar constructed during this period tended to be Victorian or eclectic in style and displayed only limited attempts to adapt to the climate or cultural setting. Design elements often appear to have been picked in a mix-and-match manner from pattern books such as Owen Jones' *The Grammar of Ornament*, 1856. Examples of these types of buildings still standing in Yangon include the Burma Railways Office [27], 1877, the Secretariat [1], 1889-1905, the Currency Department [22], circa 1900, and the Rangoon General Hospital [26], 1904-1911.

A new era of colonial architecture began with the appointment, in 1901, of a professionally trained architect [John Begg] as Consulting Architect to the Government of Bombay. The following year another architect [James Ransome] was appointed Consulting Architect to the Government of India and, by 1914, there were some 20 professionally qualified architects working in different provinces across British India. The first Consulting Architect to the Government of Burma [Henry Seton-Morris] was appointed to Yangon in 1911. Consulting Architects were expected to design important government buildings and inspect plans prepared for all public buildings. In emphasising the importance of architecture, the British had begun to realise their vision for a grander and more cohesive aesthetic across India and Myanmar; buildings became a way of imposing their rule visually as well as symbolically.

Before the Consulting Architect to the Government of Burma was appointed, buildings were designed by the Consulting Architect to the Government of India and, in the 1910s, the first batch of these was erected in Yangon. A Public Works Department report from that time noted "the great improvement in architectural work brought by these officers". Remaining examples include the Government Press [2], 1912, the Custom House [23], 1916, and the Central Telegraph Office [7], 1917.

Consulting Architects and those working in private practices met with numerous challenges in Yangon. Obtaining quality building material was a perennial problem. During the 1910s, the price of timber rose so high as to be almost prohibitive; rumours circulated that all available teakwood in Myanmar was being shipped to New Delhi for the construction of the new British capital of India. Local bricks lacked uniformity; without standard measurements, architects were unable to calculate an accurate gauge and had to repeatedly readjust the half-inch details of their designs. Often, they found it easier to ship materials from England; these included cement, steel frames, decorative elements such as the Ionic capitals for the colonnade of the New Law Courts [24], and finishings like the locks and keys for the various doors and strong rooms in the Chartered Bank [17].

Another, more serious, challenge was the waterlogged land upon which the architects had to build. As many of the building sites were located on reclaimed land, they had to conjure up innovative ways of ensuring that the buildings would be structurally sound. The Secretariat [1] was constructed upon a veritable forest of sunken *pyinkado* logs, while the Custom House [23] sits on a reinforced cement raft embedded six feet into the ground.

The most intransigent problem faced by the Consulting Architects was the demands made on them by the government. In a talk John Begg gave in London in 1920, he provided an example of the many "crass ideas" he was forced to deal with: "I remember once when the design of an important town-hall was entrusted to me, that a message was sent me from a high quarter to this effect: 'Do ask Mr. Begg, whatever he does, to make it castellated'!"

The municipal authorities also attempted to control the city's architectural development. In the early decades of the 20th century, the municipality struggled against a building boom that was being handled in large part by amateur and untrained architects. In 1908, the city had to condemn 35 buildings and order that they be either partially or totally demolished due to poor construction and use of unsafe materials. According to the law, plans for buildings to be erected within the municipal zone had to be approved by the municipal authorities. Many contractors, however, simply deposited their plans at City Hall and then started building, knowing that it would be harder for the municipality to enforce changes once the structure was complete. One municipal report noted that a great deal of the surveyor's time was spent looking at plans that "reveal a complete want of knowledge of the science of building".

In order to curb the unruly nature of construction in Yangon, the municipal authorities ended up enforcing a system whereby architects and contractors had to obtain a special license from City Hall before they were allowed to produce building plans. It was, for some, an unpopular system; The Royal Institute of British Architects (RIBA) protested that it gave the municipal authorities absolute control over the city's architectural development and were concerned about the resulting corruption and nepotism it enabled.

In 1928, the municipality cemented its control by appointing an Architectural Advisory Committee to sanction the architectural features of buildings constructed on important streets in the city. A municipal report happily noted that, within just a year, the committee had "already done much to preserve and improve the beauty of Rangoon by seeing that no ugly buildings are erected on those streets entrusted to its care".

Though the Great Depression of the 1930s curtailed building efforts in Yangon due to economic cutbacks, some of the city's grandest and most striking buildings were constructed around this time, namely the Port Authority (21), 1928, New Law Courts (24), 1931, Reserve Bank of India (9), 1939, and City Hall (4), not fully completed until 1940. These grand edifices were probably inspired by the extreme example of monumentalism on display at New Delhi, the new British capital of India. They represent a final attempt to capture a colonial aesthetic in a colony that would soon regain its independence.

"My visit to Rangoon [in 1909] gave me a most favourable impression of that city and its possibilities for future architectural development. In addition to its beautiful surroundings, its very fine parks and its well laid out cantonments, it has, what no Indian town that I have seen possesses, a well-conceived plan. With its fine wide streets, and its rectangular lay out, it has everything to encourage the hope that it will develop into a fine town. It would be difficult to spoil Rangoon entirely, but easy to miss the opportunity afforded to make it one of the finest cities in the East." — John Begg, Consulting Architect to the Government of India

KEMMENDINE
31
U WISARA ROAD
7
BAGAYA PONGYI ROAD
BOUNDARY ROAD
SHWEGONDAIN
10
28
SHWEDAGON PAGODA
1
WINDSOR ROAD
PROME ROAD
29
34
26
52
AHLONE ROAD
PAGODA ROAD
HALPIN ROAD
U WISARA ROAD
LOWER KEMMENDINE ROAD
MISSION ROAD
AHLONE
48
49
STRAND ROAD
WEST STREET
STREET
42
COMMISSIONERS ROAD
GODWIN ROAD
KEIGHLEY
43
CANAL STREET
30
DALHOUSIE ST
CHINA STREET
RANGOON RIVER

ARCHITECTS OF THE COLONIAL STATE

Henry Hoyne-Fox (1855-1905), FRIBA

Executive Engineer, Public Works Department, Burma (1882-?)
Hoyne-Fox was a prolific PWD engineer and his surviving buildings include the Secretariat (1), old Law Courts on Strand Road (replaced), and President's House (demolished).

James Ransome (1865-1944), FRIBA

Consulting Architect to the Government of India (1902-1908)
Among numerous buildings across India, Ransome designed government offices at Simla in India, and Dacca and Chittagong in Bangladesh. In Yangon, he designed the High Court (8).

John Begg (1866-1937), FRIBA

Consulting Architect to the Government of Bombay (1901-1908)
Consulting Architect to the Government of India (1908-1921)
Three of Begg's buildings survive in Yangon – Government Press (2), Telegraph Office (7), and the Custom House (23). Of the many he designed in India, the most famous is the Bombay Post Office.

Henry Seton-Morris (1869-1915), FRIBA

Consulting Architect to the Government of Burma (1911-1915)
Seton-Morris was responsible for the design of courthouses, hospitals, and offices across Myanmar. In Yangon, he designed various buildings on the University of Yangon campus.

Edgar John Pullar (1876-1929), FRIBA

Consulting Architect to the Government of Burma (1915-1916 and 1920-1925)
Pullar arrived in Yangon in 1905, having previously worked in Singapore for the prominent firm Swan & Maclaren. He set up a private practice with fellow architect Thomas Swales and maintained offices in Sofaer's Buildings (13).

Thomas Oliphant Foster (1881-1942), FRIBA

Assistant Consulting Architect to the Government of India (1913-1915)
Consulting Architect to the Government of Burma (1916-1920)
Foster began his colonial career as assistant to John Begg in India, and was then appointed to Yangon. After retiring from his government job, he opened a private practice in Yangon and designed the Port Authority (21) and New Law Courts (24).

FRIBA (Fellow of the Royal Institute of British Architects)

E ALONG STRAND ROAD

The Strand Road was the first area to be developed by the British for commerce and trade. Together with the lower block of Pansodan Street, this stretch of the Strand from Bo Aung Kyaw Street to Sule Pagoda Road is a heritage asset unparalleled in Southeast Asia.

A row of former commercial buildings that once made good use of this prime riverside location still stands on Strand Road. At the corner of Bo Aung Kyaw Street is the **Central Post Office (18)**, which was built as the office of Bulloch Brothers & Co., once one of the largest rice milling firms operating in Myanmar.

Next to it is another former trading company office that became the **British Embassy (19)** and the legendary **Strand Hotel (20)**, which has been in almost continuous operation since it first opened for business in 1901. The next building is unremarkable architecturally but once housed the famous Bombay Burmah Trading Company, a timber firm which played a pivotal role in the colonization of Myanmar. This stretch of buildings is followed by a series of large administrative offices: the **Port Authority (21)**, **Yangon Division Court (22)**, the **Custom House (23)**, and the **Yangon Division Office Complex (24)**. Finally, on the far corner of Sule Pagoda Road is the **Myanmar Economic Bank 3 (25)**, set in the once opulent offices of the Imperial Bank of India.

Most of these buildings are relatively well maintained but the area is threatened by new developments, such as the expansion of the Strand into an eight-lane road to accommodate increased traffic to and from the ports.

Local architects and urban planners are keenly interested in protecting this area together with the lower block of Pansodan Street and suggest that it could be developed along the lines of the Shanghai Bund in China. U Win Myint, a patron of the Association of Myanmar Architects, suggests that a section of the waterfront (between Bo Aung Kyaw and Pansodan streets) be converted into a riverside promenade, which would require the relocation of certain port activities currently conducted along this stretch. "We should make a feature of this area," says U Win Myint. "Now, when tourists visit the city, there's not so much for them to do – they visit the Shwedagon and Sule pagodas, do some shopping at Scott Market and then they are done. If we develop this area and Pansodan Street it could become a major tourist attraction, generating income for the developers as well as for local residents and small business enterprises in the area."

Along St[illegible]

18 CENTRAL POST OFFICE

Location: Strand Road, corner of Bo Aung Kyaw Street

Built: 1908

Architect/ Contractor: A. C. Martin & Co. (contractor)

opposite: Delightful beaux-arts portico, Post Office building

Painted maroon with cream stuccowork and rows of Lancet-arched windows, this building still retains some fine original fittings such as the beaux-arts portico and double-winged stairways in the foyer.

PAST

This building was originally designed as the office of Bulloch Brothers & Co, one of the oldest and most powerful trading firms in Myanmar. Bulloch Brothers was first established in Sittwe around 1840 and expanded to Yangon in the 1850s. Run by two brothers from Glasgow, Scotland, James and George Bulloch, the firm advertised itself as the "Largest rice millers in the East" and operated mills in Yangon, Pathein, Sittwe, and Mawlamyaing. The firm also ran a shipping line between London and Yangon, and imported hardware, salt, and other goods to Myanmar.

The original Central Post Office building, which stood on the corner of Strand Road and 32nd Street, was a delicately ornate structure of iron-filigreed grille work. The fragile building was badly damaged in the 1930 earthquake, as many of its cast-iron posts snapped. Though the Public Works Department had drawn up plans for a new and bigger Post Office, the worldwide economic depression meant that the department's funds were exceptionally low. In 1936, the state purchased this building from Bulloch Brothers together with the adjoining plot behind it to convert into a new General Post Office. New sanitation and electrical systems were installed and a sorting office was constructed on the adjoining plot.

FOREIGN MAIL
INLAND MAIL

Bulloch Brothers continued to trade in Burma until World War II but, like many foreign companies, did not return again afterwards.

During the 1930s, long before he became President of Burma in 1962, General Ne Win worked in this newly renovated building. As a post office clerk, legend has it that he was able to help his colleagues in the nationalist struggle for independence from the British by surreptitiously checking mail and telegrams, and informing them of government plans and police movements.

PRESENT

This building still functions as a busy downtown post office. At present, it is one of the few government buildings that tourists are allowed to enter without prior permission to view the interior of a colonial-era structure.

19 BRITISH EMBASSY

formerly
J. & F. GRAHAM SHIPPING CO.

Location: 80 Strand Road

Built: circa 1900

Architect/ Contractor: Thomas Swales [architect], Robinson & Mundy [contractor]

The exterior of this white four-storey building is beautifully maintained and serves as a fine example of merchant trading house architecture at the turn of the last century.

PAST

This building was originally built to house the J. & F. Graham Company, a major shipping and insurance agency that opened its offices in Rangoon in 1898. In addition to its main business, the company also dealt in imports and exports [mostly rice]. J. & F. Graham had its headquarters in Glasgow, Scotland, and had already established branches in Bombay [now Mumbai], Calcutta [now Kolkata], and Karachi, before setting up here.

An advertisement for the firm's insurance services, printed in 1922, promised its customers a thorough package that covered "fire, marine, motor accidents, and burglary [including theft by servants]".

J. & F. Graham also imported Rowntree's chocolate to Myanmar, including the plain York and Aero chocolate bars still familiar to British schoolchildren today.

After Independence, this office became the British Embassy. When the British Council library was moved from Rander House [12] the books were kept here and a side entrance was opened for access. Unlike today, the library then kept very few hours and was only open three days a week for two hours at a time. Later, in the early 1990s, the British Council was modernised and expanded to its current size.

PRESENT

This building still serves as the British Embassy and also contains the British Council library and offices, which are accessible via the side entrance.

Next door is the Australian Embassy, which was built in 1913 as an additional annex to the Strand Hotel [20].

20 THE STRAND HOTEL

Location: 92 Strand Road

Built: 1901

Architect/ Contractor: John Darwood (architect), T. N. J. Catchatoor & Co. (contractor)

Having undergone regular renovations throughout the upheavals of the past century, the Strand Hotel is the country's most finely restored colonial-era building.

PAST

In 1886, news of Great Britain's annexation of Upper Burma (as the British called northern Myanmar) rippled across the region and businessmen began clamouring for a foothold in Yangon as they foresaw the country opening up tolucrative trading opportunities. Yangon, however, had no adequate accommodation for this influx of prospectors. An Armenian family firm, known as the Sarkies Brothers, had recently opened the Raffles Hotel in Singapore and decided to search for a good location in Yangon. They eventually snagged this ideal spot, with its river view and convenient proximity to the jetty where visitors disembarked.

The plot was originally occupied by a small and shabby wooden boarding house. The owner, John Darwood, happened to be an architect and drew up plans for a new hotel according to a design by the Sarkies Brothers. The building was constructed by Tigran Nierces Joseph Catchatoor, a Turkish-Armenian contractor who was born in Yangon (and who later ended up buried around the corner from this hotel at the Armenian Cemetery on Bo Aung Kyaw Street). At the time, Catchatoor was considered one of the most experienced builders in the city; when he began his trade, most buildings were still being made of wood.

STRAND HOTEL

STRAND HOTEL.
LONG LIVE THE EMPEROR

The Sarkies Brothers commissioned a 60-room hotel, with dining room, drawing room, and six-table billiard room. The hotel was remarkable for having electric lighting, made possible through an in-house generator [at that time, most of the city was lit only by candles and kerosene lamps]. A French chef was hired to design a menu of European specialties. The finest ingredients were sailed in from around the world; through their Persian connections, the Sarkies Brothers imported caviar from the Caspian Sea.

The hotel was an instant success and soon became the best-known hotel in Myanmar. The Sarkies Brothers had hit on a winning blend of Asian and European hospitality that would influence the hotel business throughout the region for years to come; Raffles is still one of Asia's finest hotels, as is another Sarkies Brothers establishment, the Eastern & Oriental Hotel [the E&O], in Penang, Malaysia.

So many guests flocked to the Strand Hotel that, in 1913, the brothers had to build an annex next door. This building was later reserved for officers of aircrews flying for Imperial Airways and the British Overseas Airways Corporation [which would eventually become part of British Airways]. Later still, the annex became and still remains the Australian Embassy.

In 1925, the Sarkies Brothers sold the hotel to a local Armenian restaurant owner called Peter Bugalar Aratoon, who ran the fashionable restaurant Silver Grill [see page 73]. The hotel was totally renovated in 1927 and a swimming pool was built at the rear. The concrete driveway and portico that still stands today was added in front of the building.

In 1937, another round of renovations were conducted and the number of rooms was increased to 100. The swimming pool was covered over and an extension was added behind the hotel, opening up a new entrance on Lewis [now Seikkanthar] Street.

During World War II, the Japanese took over the hotel and brought over staff from the Imperial Hotel in Tokyo to run the establishment. The building was renamed the Yamato Hotel but was not well cared for and the lobby was wrecked by Japanese officers stabling their horses in the bar.

When Aratoon returned after the war, he found the hotel strewn with rubbish and discovered that an unexploded bomb had fallen straight through the roof in his office. Once again, the hotel was thoroughly refurbished and, in 1949, it was sold to the Steel Brothers Company, heralding another decade of successful business throughout the 1950s.

below left: The Strand Hotel decorated for the Coronation of King Edward, Emperor of India, in 1902, just a year after it opened for business

In 1963, the hotel was nationalised under the socialist government and its days of luxury were temporarily suspended as foreign travelers were restricted to visiting the country for only a day or two. By the time Tony Wheeler, the founder of Lonely Planet guide books, stayed here in the 1970s, the hotel was much deteriorated and was host to more rats than guests. Wheeler wrote, "Both the bar and restaurant close at 9 p.m., but a small cache of Mandalay Beer from the People's Brewery is kept behind the reception desk should you wish to continue drinking. By 11 p.m. you are likely to be feeling pretty lonely in the lounge area, though, just the occasional Strand rat scampering across the floor to keep you company."

In his 1979 guide book, Wheeler recommended that guests choose the US$11.50 rooms on the second floor as they were better than those on the first floor, "in as much as the tatty and dilapidated second-floor bathrooms are at least less tatty and dilapidated than those on the first floor."

Then, in 1990, an enterprising joint venture was formed between the Myanmar government and Indonesian hotelier Adrian Zecha (founder of Aman Resorts). The hotel was closed for three years of renovations, though the annex behind the main building remained operational as a basic hotel. After an extensive face-lift, the hotel reopened in 1993 with 32 fully renovated rooms and has remained a famous destination for well-heeled tourists ever since.

PRESENT

Today, the Strand Hotel is part of the global GHM Luxury Hotels chain, which also manages exclusive hotels in Miami, Bali, and Vietnam, among other destinations.

The Strand Hotel in Yangon, together with the Governor's Residence hotel on Taw Win Road, serves as good examples of hotel businesses that have made a feature of renovating old properties.

A VIEW FROM THE STRAND

In the early 1900s, the British painter R. Talbot Kelly sat at his balcony in the Strand Hotel observing the city's street life, echoes of which can still be seen today:

"Here is a water carrier, whose terracotta water jars are slung from a bamboo carried on his shoulder, another man bears on his head a tray upon which a charcoal fire is cooking a strong smelling 'tit-bit' some hungry labourer will presently enjoy. Huge baskets of coconuts or vegetables, gaudily painted calicoes and haberdashery, cheap knives and looking-glasses, and baskets of cool melons, are some of the articles carried across the shoulders of the peddlers, while porters pass to and fro bearing huge burdens from one warehouse to another."

21 PORT AUTHORITY

Location: Strand Road, corner of Pansodan Street

Built: 1928

Architect/ Contractor: Thomas Oliphant Foster (architect), Clark & Greig (contractor)

This stunning building has many unique features, including its square corner tower, wave-inspired stuccowork, and the bas-relief sculptures of sailing vessels carved high upon its walls.

PAST

By 1910, the port at Yangon had become the third largest in the British Empire and this building was built to signify that importance. As the port is served by tidal waters, its early development was challenging and costly and much of it was pushed through by the Board of Port Commissioners who believed that the city owed its success in maritime trade to the accessibility and expansiveness of its port.

Day-to-day tasks of the Port Authority were to maintain, mark, and light the channel and the harbour and maintain moorings, anchorages, and public wharves and jetties. The Commission was also responsible for controlling the movement of shipping and the unloading and storing of cargo on public wharves.

opposite:
Building details, Port Authority

This building replaced an older Port Authority building constructed in 1865, which was condemned as unsafe and demolished in 1925. The foundation stone of the new building was laid on 17 March 1926 by His Excellency Sir Spencer Harcourt Butler, Governor of Burma. Concrete Monolith piles were driven into the soil and a steel framework was erected by the British steel company Dorman Long, which was based in Middlesborough, England, but had an office in Yangon.

The architect, Thomas Oliphant Foster (1881-1942), had begun his career in the East as Assistant Consulting Architect to the Government of India in 1913, serving under John Begg. In 1916, he moved to Yangon after being appointed the Consulting Architect to the Government of Burma. Foster resigned from that position in 1920 to set up a private practice in Yangon from which he designed two very prominent buildings on the Strand, this one and the New Law Courts (24) nearby.

That this building survives today is quite incredible given that Yangon's port was targeted during World War II, both by Japanese bombings and the British "scorched earth" policy of destroying anything that might be useful to incoming Japanese forces.

In 1954, the Commission was renamed the Board of Management for the Port of Rangoon, and in 1972 it became the Burma Ports Corporation. In 1989, it took its present name as the Myanmar Port Authority.

PRESENT

Though the Port Authority is still using the building, most of its activities have shifted to another office and it has been reported that all state-owned port facilities will soon be privatised.

The work of the Port Authority has contributed much to the development of Yangon and should not go unacknowledged. This building stands as a key and instantly recognizable element of the riverside cityscape – a view which, seen from the river, has hardly changed since the building was first constructed.

Next door, at 104 Strand Road between the Port Authority and the Strand Hotel, is the Myanmar Airways Office. This seemingly undistinguished building has been stripped bare of any architectural ornamentation but it was originally the famous Bombay Burmah Trading Corporation office. It was a dispute between this company and Myanmar's last monarch, King Thibaw, that led to the third Anglo-Burmese War and the final British annexation of Myanmar.

22 YANGON DIVISION COURT

formerly
CURRENCY DEPARTMENT

Location:
1 Pansodan Street, corner of Strand Road

Built: circa 1900

Architect/ Contractor:
A. C. Martin (contractor)

This evocative pastel blue-green building featuring octagonal corner domes was bombed during World War II; the damage is still visible on the Bank Street side of the building.

PAST

This building has a unique footprint, as it has three asymmetrical wings that effectively wrap the building around the block and the neighbouring Custom House. It was built in stages, with the extension on the east added in 1905-1907 to cater to the needs of the expanding Currency Department and to create offices for the Accountant-General of Burma. As such, this building housed the most influential offices in British Burma. The office oversaw the collection of government revenue, which came from opium (importation and legal sales), salt, custom duties, railways, post office, telegraphs, tributes, military works, and major irrigation projects.

During construction, a conflict broke out over this building and the Custom House and the latter was forced to demolish part of its bonded warehouse, a corrugated iron structure that was blocking ventilation and lighting in the Currency Department's new extension.

The entire structure originally stretched for a full block along Bank Street but the Bank Street wing was bombed during World War II. A low-rise structure was built in place of the missing wing as an office for administering government pensions.

This building is one of the oldest masonry structures still standing in the city and has always been vulnerable. In 1908 a portion of the façade along Strand Road collapsed and took over a year to rebuild. Then, in 1930, a long wall was badly damaged and had to be rebuilt with additional supports.

After Independence, the building served as a small claims civil court and later, during the socialist period, as a juvenile court.

PRESENT

This building currently houses the Yangon [South and West] Division Court. The bombed area behind the building is still a pensions office. In front of it, temporary structures have been built for teashops and food stalls that cater to lawyers and office workers attending to court matters in the nearby courts. There are also photocopy shops and "scribes" who offer typewriting and computing services for clients needing to fill in legal forms.

The Currency Department today, showing the wing that was destroyed by bombing raids during World War II and the Custom House in the background

POTENTIAL

Yangon architect U Sun Oo, Vice President of the Association of Myanmar Architects, would like to see the space behind this court building cleared and turned into a miniature public park with organised facilities for teashops and food vendors. "Because it was not rebuilt after the bomb damage during the war, it is one of the most interesting buildings in the city today," he says. "It has become frozen in time – the same architectural scene just after the bomb was dropped is the same scene we see today."

23 CUSTOM HOUSE

Location: 132 Strand Road, between Pansodan Street and Mahabandoola Garden Street

Built: 1912-1916

Architect/ Contractor: John Begg (architect), Clark & Greig (contractor)

This large brick building, which features an elegant white tower and two-faced clock above the entranceway, is yet another impressive example of colonial administrative architecture.

PAST

Located just near the Sule Pagoda Wharf, this building was ideally situated to monitor duties on goods coming into the country. It was designed by the Scottish architect John Begg who was Consulting Architect to the Government of India (see page 31) and erected by the contracting firm Clark & Greig (see page 55) – the same architect-and-engineer team that built the Telegraph Office (7).

The roof of the old Custom House, located on this same plot, had been deteriorating for years and leaked so badly during each monsoon season that the Public Works Department eventually gave up patching it and erected an entirely new roof of corrugated iron set on an iron frame above the original roof. Early sketches for a much-needed new Custom House executed by the Department failed to meet government expectations and the job was handed over to John Begg.

Begg completed his drawings in 1911 and, as soon as financial estimates were finalised, construction began the following year. The building presented the common Yangon challenge of how to erect a heavy structure on unstable soil. In this instance, foundations were dug down to an average depth of six feet and consisted of a reinforced concrete raft two feet thick with grills to carry the building's stanchions. The superstructure above it was steel-framed and encased in brick. The steelwork was done by the Dorman Long company and fitted together at their headquarters in Middlesborough, England, before being sent out to Yangon.

Begg's original design included a clock tower but the tower was later modified when it was decided to use a two-faced bracket clock on the front wall instead. The top floor was designed with built-in apartments for Customs staff, some of whom needed to be on call 24 hours a day. These were long and narrow residences built like railway carriages with all the rooms opening onto a corridor that ran the length of the apartment.

Under the British, the Custom House had a team of Preventative Officers known informally as the "Rummaging Staff" who searched ships and transit sheds for contraband goods. As with any big port, smuggling attempts were constant and people were caught on a daily basis at the transit sheds or wharf gates attempting to remove packages before they had been cleared by Customs.

Bill Tydd, a British Assistant Collector of Customs in the late 1930s, recalled the drudge of searching ships, a process that was dirty and tiresome and could take the Rummage Team more than a day. Tydd was often astounded by the ingenuity and trouble taken to conceal contraband drugs, gold, gems, and other goods. He found them hidden "behind bulkheads, inside ventilators, lifeboats, lavatory cisterns, bath and washbasin drainage S bends, in remote spaces in cargo holds, the list is endless and they all had to be looked into". He once found a substantial amount of opium under a great heap of coal in a fuel bunker on an old ship trading between China and India: "The laborious task of having to remove tons of coal before recovering the cakes of opium in their protective bags appeared to be no deterrent to that determined gang [of Custom House rummagers]."

Tydd also noted that the wealth involved in the maritime trade through Yangon grew steadily. "By 1942, Customs duty revenue had overtaken Land Tax revenue, until then by far the largest source of income for the Government."

PRESENT

The building has remained in almost constant use and is in fairly good condition – even the clock, installed almost a century ago, is still in use.

THE GLASGOW-YANGON ARCHITECTURAL AXIS

The use of Scottish architects (such as John Begg) and the large number of Scottish firms doing business in Yangon has left its legacy architecturally, as the city bears a striking resemblance to many buildings of a similar period in Glasgow. Foreign firms operating in Yangon that had their headquarters in Glasgow include Bulloch Brothers & Co. (18), J. & F. Graham & Co. (19), Finlay, Fleming & Co. (10), and the Irrawaddy Flotilla Company (14).

left: The Burmah Oil Company (10) had its head office in this building on West George Street, Glasgow © Crown Copyright: RCAHMS

right: The office block where the Irrawaddy Flotilla Company (14) had its head office, Bothwell Street, Glasgow © Crown Copyright: RCAHMS

24 YANGON DIVISION OFFICE COMPLEX

formerly
NEW LAW COURTS

Location: Strand Road, east corner of Sule Pagoda Road

Built: 1927-1931

Architect/ Contractor: Thomas Oliphant Foster (architect), United Engineers (contractor)

This massive and formidable building dominates the block on which it was built with a colonnade of Ionic columns that stands three floors high and seems to stretch endlessly along the Strand.

PAST

Built by the Public Works Department to house the city's new law courts, this enormous steel-framed structure replaced an earlier court building that had been designed by the PWD engineer Henry Hoyne-Fox and was demolished in 1926. The enormous steel framework required almost 3,000 tons of steel and was constructed by the steel manufacturing company Dorman Long from Middlesbrough, England. According to an article in the *Rangoon Gazette* written at the time of the building's completion, it was the city's finest and most up-to-date building and drawings for its design were hung at the Royal Academy in London.

The architect, Thomas Oliphant Foster, was undoubtedly inspired by the designs that Edwin Lutyens had been preparing for New Delhi, the new capital the British were building in India. In 1914, Foster had worked as an assistant to John Begg and been seconded to the special Delhi Committee tasked with dreaming up a new capital. Foster spent six months working under Lutyens and, like many young architects of the time, replicated his use of Palladian Classicism and sense of monumentalism.

top right: The New Law Courts while under construction, showing the steel frame, 1928

The foundations required 600 Simplex piles and the building was erected fairly rapidly until delays were met in 1929 when the 22 Ionic capitols ordered for the colonnade from England failed to arrive on schedule.

During World War II, when the Japanese occupied Myanmar, this building became a notorious and much-feared establishment as the Japanese secret police [known as the Kempetai] used it as an interrogation centre and prison. After 1974, the building was used for a few years as an imposing headquarters for the Burma Socialist Programme Party [BSPP].

PRESENT

This building now houses the collective law courts for Yangon's North and East divisions, as well as police posts.

A series of eclectic bas-relief symbols survive on the building's back wall along Bank Street. These recurring images include a peacock, sword, and five-pointed star. As the star looks like the Star of David, people used to refer informally to this building as the "Jewish Building". Other features include the ornate steel entry doors and a plaque on one of columns marking the foundation stone laid on 3 March 1927 by the British Governor, Sir Harcourt Butler.

THE LUTYENS THEORY OF COLONIAL ARCHITECTURE

Edwin Lutyens believed there were two ways of building in India. One was to parade buildings "in fancy dress" as at a costume ball, mixing dates and styles. The other was to "build as an Englishman dressed for the climate", conscious only that the tailor was of Agra or Benares, and not of Savile Row or Petticoat Lane. The latter was the method Lutyens preferred.

Architect's drawing of the New Law Courts, 1926, Thomas O. Foster

25 MYANMAR ECONOMIC BANK 3

formerly
IMPERIAL BANK OF INDIA

Location: 1/19 Sule Pagoda Road, west corner of Strand Road

Built: 1914

Architect/ Contractor: Unknown

This opulent but now faded building with an elaborate corner tower once housed the Imperial Bank of India and was linked to the city's main financial quarters on Merchant Street.

PAST

Originally home to the Bank of Bengal, this building later became the Imperial Bank of India after the Indian Presidency banks of Bengal, Bombay, and Madras merged in 1921. The Bank of Bengal first set up operations in Yangon in 1861 and, unlike many other commercial banks, provided capital to the Indian *chettiars* [Indians from Chettinad in Tamil Nadu who became known as moneylenders throughout the British Empire].

After both India and Myanmar regained their independence from Britain, the bank became known as the State Bank of India. In the 1950s, other offices were housed in this building such as the Swedish consulate and the Burma Match Company. On 23 February 1963, along with all over private banks in Myanmar, the State Bank of India was nationalised and became People's Bank 8.

The *Handbook on Burma*, published by the Directorate of Information in 1968, attempts to explain the Revolutionary Council's rationale for nationalising all the

Building details and, bottom left, the Imperial Bank of India abandoned during World War II, Frank Bond, 1945

country's private banks: "This step was inevitable under the socialist economic aims and objectives. Private banks were custodians of public deposits which they loaned to private capitalists. The volume of business was substantial and their annual profits enormous. Moreover, by being the only channel for import-export transactions of the country ... these banks controlled about one-third of the gross national product. Hence, it was undesirable that such a strong hold on the national economy should remain in private hands."

PRESENT

Today, this building is the state-owned Myanmar Economic Bank 3. At the Sule Pagoda Road entrance, it is still possible to make out the words "of India" beneath flaking layers of successive paintwork.

YANGON RENOVATIONS: SUCCESSES & CHALLENGES

A small but growing number of entrepreneurs in Yangon are choosing to restore colonial-era buildings for business purposes. So far, old properties have been transformed into popular restaurants and bars, an elegant bank building, a funky art gallery, and the office and printing press of a weekly news journal.

One of the early pioneers of restoration in Yangon after the country began to open up to foreign investment in the 1990s was 50th Street Bar & Grill, which opened its doors in 1997. The building had been constructed in 1906 and was occupied by Burmese traders who benefited from its proximity to the river. For co-owner Anthony Alderson, location was one of the key motivating factors in choosing this building – many old properties occupy prime settings in or near the city centre.

The project was full of challenges. Being close to the river meant the building was susceptible to rising damp and much of the initial investment went into upgrading the electrical system and water supply. The structure also had to be reinforced to allow for a restaurant on the first floor.

50th Street has now been running for over a decade and is popular with the expatriate crowd and well-heeled Burmese in search of Western fare and atmosphere. "There's nothing like a bit of heritage to build a hospitality business around," says Alderson. "Keeping the past is a great starting point for any development in a country where people have visions of the past."

Façade of 50th Street Bar & Grill

Interior of 50th Street Bar & Grill

For Daw Phyu Phyu, one of the three partners who own and operate Yangon's Monsoon Restaurant & Bar (picture overleaf), old buildings are all about atmosphere. "We wanted to recreate the atmosphere of the colonial era," she says. "So we decorated the building with warm colours, used indirect lighting, and installed ceiling fans and rattan furniture. The cutlery and crockery were also carefully chosen to match the building's interior."

Set in a row of shop houses on Theinbyu Road, Monsoon is an elegant restaurant that serves up Southeast Asian cuisines, including Myanmar and Thai dishes. When the trio took over the three-storey building, it was being used as the office of a tour company. The partnership renovated the entire structure from top to bottom to create a restaurant on the ground and first floors and a shop on the top floor. The renovation was carefully planned so as not to disturb the original design, though walls were knocked down to create more space.

The process cost more than it would have to redo a modern property but Daw Phyu Phyu believes it was worth it. She explains that the unique look as well as the colonial décor and setting attracts tourists and foreigners while the thick walls and high ceilings help keep the building cool and provide favourable acoustics for music. "I'm also pleased and proud to be preserving the rich history of Yangon," she says.

Gallery 65 in Yaw Min Gyi Road is a small art gallery hosting collective and solo exhibitions that focus on contemporary Myanmar paintings and sculpture by both established and emerging artists. The gallery's promise is to display contemporary

Façade of Monsoon Restaurant & Bar

art that is "always fresh, new and original". What makes Gallery 65 unique is that it is set in a colonial-era house When owner U Min Lwin was searching for a venue in which to open a gallery, he eventually settled on his own family home.

The house is a picturesque two-storey residence in characteristic Burmese colonial style with a cream-coloured concrete base and a dark wood first floor. It is now one of the last of its kind on the street; it was originally part of a group of four similar houses but two were destroyed in World War II and the other was sold to a property developer who replaced it with an apartment block. The renovation involved converting the downstairs area into an exhibition space of about 1,500 square feet that could be properly air-conditioned. "It was definitely hard work," says U Min Lwin. "When you're dealing with an old house, you start with one thing and then something else comes up that needs to be fixed."

Looking beyond the challenges, U Min Lwin says there are plenty of benefits to having his gallery in an old building. The gallery benefits from a sense of space and good lighting afforded by the old-fashioned high ceilings. It also attracts visitors due to its atmospheric setting. And business has been booming – in the first year and a half after the gallery opened in May 2010, it held 20 separate shows and was booked up well into the following year.

"Successful heritage work brings life back to historical buildings by giving them a contemporary use rather than creating frozen artefacts of the past," says Amelie Chai of SPINE Architects, Yangon. SPINE has been involved in a number of renovation projects around the city, including the *Myanmar Times* office and printing press on Bo Aung Kyaw Street, the head office of Max Myanmar on Ah Lan Pya Pagoda Road, and the Yuzana Tea retail outlet and residence on Na Wa Day Street.

Gallery 65, front and interior

Max Myanmar offices, SPINE Architects

Architecturally speaking, a restoration project can present plenty of hurdles. Chai points out that safety standards are a critical component that needs to be addressed in each project. "Buildings built a hundred years ago have different safety standards than we do today," she says. "There was no seismic contingent then and buildings now must meet greater structural loading requirements. We also should be aware of changes in our perceptions of quality. A lot of old buildings are no longer conducive to today's living standards. When we talk about preservation, we have to be careful not to preserve things that have become unsafe and unsuitable."

By far the biggest hurdle to any restoration project is financial – it costs money to turn an old building into a modern venue. When construction and renovation costs are added to the high cost of land in Yangon, the final price tag can be exorbitant.

Yet, there can also be unexpected rewards. When restoration workers chipped away the plaster walls of the building that became 50th Street Bar & Grill, they uncovered an intricate brick wall made with bricks imported from England almost a century ago; the bricks are now a key feature of the restaurant's design. Amelie Chai refers to the stripping down process in a restoration

Yuzana Tea, interior and exterior, SPINE Architects

project as working through "a collage of layers". She says, "We might knock down a false ceiling and find that it has been hiding the higher vaulted ceiling of the original structure. Part of the process involves making these kinds of surprising discoveries."

There are growing numbers of expertly renovated buildings in Yangon. Among them is the Acacia Tea Salon [52 Saya San Road], founded in 2008 and set in a refurbished private home. With its refined white-and-pistachio interior and rosewood furniture, this restaurant serves up epicurean fare in an idealised colonial setting. Local staff have been trained by a French chef and there is a resident Thai chef, a veteran of 5-star hotel restaurants in Thailand. Harking back to the cosmopolitan days of "old Rangoon", the bakery produces fine French patisseries and imports tea, chocolate, and jams from around the world.

In addition to these smaller businesses, the city also has a handful of hotels that have made use of renovated buildings such as the Governor's Residence, a teakwood mansion constructed as a government guesthouse in the 1920s, the Savoy Hotel, which was converted from a doctor's residence, and the legendary Strand Hotel [20].

F ELSEWHERE IN YANGON

There are a great number and variety of impressive colonial-era buildings beyond the city centre. Outside of religious structures and private homes, the most exceptional of these include the **Yangon General Hospital (26)** on Bogyoke Aung San Road, the nearby building that once served as the **Burma Railways Company (27)** office, and the former **Pegu Club (28)**, on Sagawa Street – the latter two are the oldest British buildings still standing in Yangon. Just across Pyay Road from the old Pegu Club is the residential apartment block, Prome Court, which later became the **Ministry of Foreign Affairs (29)**. Near Inya Lake on Kaba Aye Pagoda Road is the old Ministry of Culture building, which was originally built as a lavish private mansion; though it currently houses the **State Fine Arts School (30)**, it is still often referred to as the Chin Tsong Palace.

26 YANGON GENERAL HOSPITAL

formerly
RANGOON GENERAL HOSPITAL

Location: Bogyoke Aung San Road, between Lanmadaw Street and Shwedagon Pagoda Road

Built: 1904-1911

Architect/ Contractor: Henry Hoyne-Fox (architect), Bagchi & Co. (contractor)

This rambling hospital, with its bevelled domes and multiple wings, retains the old-world feel of a Victorian sanatorium.

PAST

The city's first General Hospital, built in 1873, was made of teak and by the early 1890s had become too cramped for the number of patients it was treating; patients had to be accommodated outside on the verandahs due to lack of room in the wards. Herbert Thirkell-White (Governor of Burma 1905-1910) also noted that the wooden structure had become "saturated by generations of microbes [which] was a disgrace to civilization".

A site for a new and larger hospital was found at the present spot, though it required the relocation of the Phayre Museum (the exhibits of which now form part of the National Museum collection) and the Agri-Horticultural Gardens, which were moved to the grounds of the current zoo.

The plans were drawn up by the Public Works Department's Executive Engineer, Henry Hoyne-Fox (though he would not live to see its completion). According to his design, the main building was 700 feet long, three stories high, and fitted with all the "latest modern improvements" in medical services, including operating theatres with electricity and anesthesia rooms.

The hospital floor was the first in Myanmar to be made with reinforced concrete, and was topped with marble and tile flooring. The walls were made from plastered brick with tile dados and the ceilings were of stamped steel.

By 1909, the main building was completed and in partial occupation. The following year was spent adding modern fixtures including the machinery required for electric lifts, ventilation, heating, laundry, and operation of the *punkah*-style fans [see page 138]. The administrative block and other structures within the compound, such as the Matron's accommodation and the morgue, were designed by Henry Seton-Morris, Consulting Architect to the Government of Burma, and completed in 1915.

John Begg, Consulting Architect to the Government of India, who saw the building as it was nearing completion while he was on a trip to Yangon, was as unimpressed with it as he had been with the High Court [8]: "Rather too much 'design' has been expended on certain portions of [its] external appearance. A hospital ward can hardly be too plain and business-like. Nor is the exterior very pleasing after all. The colour scheme of light red brick and yellow plaster is distinctly unhappy."

Still, the completed hospital had over 500 beds and offered all the latest in medical technology. Most cases treated involved common diseases such as malaria, tuberculosis, and typhoid, though doctors also gained plenty of experience in treating wounds caused by the *dah* [knife], a commonly used weapon.

Façade detail, Yangon General Hospital

CONTRIBUTIONS TO GLOBAL SCIENCE

Among the medical staff at this hospital was Major Ernst Reinhold Rost, who set up the first medical laboratory in Yangon to study the cultivation of the bacillus of leprosy. The resulting research contributed to an international effort to develop a leprosy vaccine. Rost went on to pen a book published in 1930 called *The Nature of Consciousness*, a study of Buddhist psychology [i.e., meditation] and its relation to modern science, the research for which would have been carried out in this hospital.

PRESENT

While this hospital was highly modern a century ago it is now out of date as a medical establishment, though the doctors and nurses who work within its walls are fond of the old building. "I love to work there," says one doctor, "and the location is also very good for most people. I love the old building and believe that it could be renovated to incorporate modern facilities."

The surrounding neighbourhood has a number of both old and new medical facilities. Diagonally across the Lanmadaw-Bogyoke Aung San intersection is a medical training school known as the Institute of Medicine, built by the Burmese architect U Tha Tun, who is considered one of the first architects in Myanmar along with Sithu U Tin [see pages 40-43]. On the corner of Bogyoke Aung San Road and Pyay Road is the New Yangon General Hospital, built during the socialist period with Japanese aid.

KEEPING COOL

In the days before electricity, these office buildings were generally constructed as large and airy spaces, and recessed windows were shaded by grass mats that were routinely wetted to cool the air that passed through them. R. Talbot Kelly, a British painter who travelled through Myanmar in the early 20th century, described the method by which the buildings of the "sahib" [as British rulers were addressed in India] were kept cool: "Slung from the ceiling in long rows over tables or desks are the *punkah*, or fans, which a *punkah wallah* outside in the verandah pulls to and fro with a rope in order to keep the hot air moving, and prevent the flies and mosquitoes from settling."

27 FORMER BURMA RAILWAYS COMPANY

Location: corner of Sule Pagoda Road and Bogyoke Aung San Road

Built: 1877

Architect/ Contractor: Unknown

This elegant U-shaped building with its filigreed awnings is unique for its use of laterite blocks on the ground floor and is one of the oldest administrative buildings remaining in Yangon.

PAST

This building was constructed as the headquarters of the state-run Burma Railways, which later became a private company that leased the country's railway system from the government in 1896. It was the largest commercial undertaking in the country and the railway system did much to facilitate trade and open up access throughout Myanmar. When the company took over the outfit, the country had 886 miles of single line and 134 miles of sidings; within just over a decade the track had been almost doubled to 1,529 miles with 329 miles of sidings.

The entire administration of the country's railway system was controlled from this building, which also contained offices for the General Manager of the Railways Board, the Chief Engineer, Traffic Manager, and Controller of Railway Accounts. In addition to these offices, the catering and advertising departments were located here. Ads were good business for the Burma Railways Company, which boasted in 1925 that over three million people would see advertisements displayed on its station platforms, refreshment stands, waiting rooms, book stalls, and timetables.

The company suffered enormous losses during World War II; records show that it lost 320 of 354 locomotives, 7,000 of 9,000 goods wagons, and almost all 1,000 passenger coaches. Some 200 major bridges were damaged and one million sleepers torn up. The original Rangoon Central Railway Station was almost completely destroyed during the bombing raids of World War II and the present station was constructed to replace it in the 1950s.

PRESENT

This building is now located within the compound of the Grand Mee Ya Hta Executive Residences and is in a semi-derelict state. In 1992, when the building served as an office for the Ministry of Railways, Serge Pun & Associates (Myanmar) Ltd. signed a 30-year lease on the building. Part of their agreement was the construction of a new building which the Ministry moved into in 1994. Since then, this building has been empty. Plans were made to convert the premises into a high-end office complex with a coffee shop, bakery, and garden teashop on the ground floor but these were shelved due to the Asian financial crisis in 1997. Partners involved in the potential venture are currently discussing future options for the building.

"The city of Yangon is an old city with an architectural heritage that we are enormously proud of," says Serge Pun of Serge Pun & Associates. "The old

Panoramic view of the now dilapidated Burma Railways Company office

railway headquarters had such an impact on Myanmar's transportation industry. I envisage the building being restored to its original design, with care taken to use high quality construction materials and traditional handiwork. My desire is to bring the glory back to the building so it will once again be a place where people can come and celebrate their special and memorable occasions."

POTENTIAL

The prime location and structure of this building are conducive to a number of different purposes. One suggestion is to make good use of the high ceilings and many windows by opening a series of private art galleries on the ground floor with studios for artists and sculptors or a training school on the upper floors. Several large hotels are located in this neighbourhood and Bogyoke Aung San Market is just a block away, which means that plenty of tourists visit this area.

In 2000, Chaw Kalyar and Khin Htet Htet Zaw, who were then architect students, won an Honourable Mention in an international student competition entitled "Sustainable Building for 2000". Their design for this building proposed that it be used as a modern office block in the central business district. They submitted a plan for an energy-efficient building that made the most of the thick brick walls and natural ventilation system to cool the offices.

28 FORMER PEGU CLUB

Location: Sagawa Street, off Pyay Road, opposite Russian Embassy

Built: 1882

Architect/ Contractor: Unknown

As the most exclusive British club in Burma, this building was often referred to as the real seat of power in the country. Made predominately of teak, it is one of the oldest British-built buildings still standing in Yangon.

PAST

Founded in 1871 within the military cantonment in Yangon, the Pegu Club moved to its present location just over a decade later. The club inhabited a large compound that contained tennis courts, residential apartments, and a clubhouse. The clubhouse had a billiards room, dining rooms, card rooms, reading rooms, and a well-stocked bar, which was the origin of the Pegu Club Cocktail. By 1930, the Pegu Club Cocktail (a tribute to the favourite colonial tipple, Gin and Rose's Lime Juice) was a worldwide phenomenon; Harry Craddock, the famous American barman at the Savoy Hotel in London, wrote in his book *The Savoy Cocktail Book* that the Pegu Club Cocktail "has travelled, and is asked for, around the world".

Of the city's three main clubs (the Pegu, Gymkhana, and Boat Club), the Pegu Club was the most prestigious. Its rules stated that "all gentlemen interested in general society are eligible", but in practice membership was difficult to wrangle. Most members were government officials, officers of the British

D. A. Ahuja's postcard of the Pegu Club in its hey day

army, and wealthy or well-connected professional men. In 1910, the club had 350 members, 25 of whom lived on the premises. Such was the caliber of its members that the government was sometimes jokingly referred to as "the Pegu Club government", in reference to the way club members were believed to influence the policy of the administration.

The club was strictly segregated and did not allow Asian members; even Anglo-Burmese of mixed parentage were prohibited from joining. It was, in short, the sort of "gin palace" so artfully disparaged by George Orwell in his novel *Burmese Days*.

By the late 1930s the Pegu Club and its members were already considered a relic of by-gone times. R. Raven-Hart, a British adventurer who travelled along the Ayeyarwaddy River by canoe, stopped off at the club and wrote that it was worth a visit just as any Paleolithic exhibition was worth visiting, in order to see "what used to be alive". He advised visitors to use the club for "an expert study of the fossils of Burma" and described the types that might be found there: "One of the commonest is characterised by its belief that Burma is part of India. It expects the Burman to understand Hindustani as it speaks it, it interlards its conversations with Hindustani words ... Needless to say it glories in a complete ignorance of the country it lives in, of its religion, history, and customs; it is interesting to meet and pleasant to forget."

During World War II, officers of the Japanese Imperial Army used the premises as a private club and a British intelligence report at the time noted that geisha were brought here from Japan to entertain the soldiers. When the Allied forces recaptured Yangon, Britain's Royal Air Force officers commandeered the club.

In the post-war years, the club was finally opened to Burmese though reportedly few bothered to visit. A Shan princess who visited in the 1950s describes how the club still retained a colonial atmosphere even in an independent Myanmar: "Its long verandahs provided cool and silent shade, while its polished teak bars never ran out of ice cold beer, Singapore slings, pink gins or whisky. In the shadows were the Boys [Indian staff], still Boys even if they were 50 or 60 years old, who stood quietly in the background, always ready to anticipate a need and to refill an empty glass."

The building was eventually nationalised during the socialist era and put to use as a military audit office and a dormitory for government staff.

PRESENT

Today, the main clubhouse is no longer in use but policemen and their families reside in the residential homes and in newer one-storey buildings that have been constructed along the edges of the compound.

The club building is badly deteriorated. With the exception of one meeting hall that is kept padlocked and sporadically cleaned, the rest of the building has been left to fall into disrepair. Floorboards on the first floor have rotted through, wooden staircases have become dangerous to use, and the parquet flooring in the ground floor dance hall has been picked away by vandals.

This building is not on the YCDC list of protected buildings and its future is uncertain.

POTENTIAL

As the Pegu Club has such a long history and social connection with the colonial period, it would be a unique historical attraction for tourists and could be included on day tours of Yangon.

Though the building would need extensive renovation, Daw Moe Moe Lwin, Secretary of the Association of Myanmar Architects, says, "It could be converted into a hotel – perhaps incorporating a modern hotel building in the compound, which is quite large, and using the old building as a lobby, dining and bar area."

Interiors of the Pegu Club today

TALES OF THE RAJ

Rudyard Kipling, author and unofficial poet laureate of the British Raj, spent an evening at the Pegu Club in 1889. Here, he met men directly involved in the recent takeover of Upper Burma, as northern Myanmar was called by the British. In his diary at the time, Kipling quoted a friend pointing out the characters at the bar: "See that man over there. He was cut over the head the other day at Zoungloung-goo. Awfully tough man. That chap next to him has been on the dacoit-hunt for about a year. He broke up Boh Mango's Gang: caught the Boh in a paddy field, y'know..."

By the time Kipling left the club, his head was "ringing with stories of battle, murder, and sudden death". Later, he wrote his famous poem 'Mandalay' inspired, perhaps, by the Pegu Club banter.

Exterior and interiors of the Pegu Club today

29 FORMER MINISTRY OF FOREIGN AFFAIRS

originally
PROME COURT

Location: Pyay Road, corner of Sagawa Street

Built: 1921-1922

Architect/ Contractor: Clark & Greig (contractor)

This three-storey building was originally designed as a well-appointed residential complex for members of the colonial administration.

PAST

Originally called Prome Court, this building contained 28 flats that were reserved for British government staff and was built conveniently close to the Pegu Club (28) so that residents could make use of the recreational facilities there. For some years before its construction, housing had been a problem in Yangon due to the increase in the number of male European staff after World War I. To meet the ris ng demand, Prome Court was rapidly erected; the land was purchased in 1920, plans were drawn up and sanctioned by the government that same year, construction began the following, and the complex was completed in 1922.

The author Maurice Collis (1889-1973) lived here during his last years in Myanmar when he was working as the District Magistrate of Yangon. Collis was inordinately fond of the country and penned numerous books about his time here (such as *Into Hidden Burma* and *Trials in Burma*) along with novels (*She Was a Queen*) and histories (*Siamese White* and *The Land of the*

Great Image) set in Myanmar that are still read today. In his book *Trials in Burma*, which describes his time as District Magistrate, he mentions living on an upper floor of Prome Court from where he could see the Pegu Club, the "centre of official gossip". Collis returned to England in April 1931: "The East can be too exotic," he wrote. "There comes a time when one longs for buttercups and the hedges of May."

In February 1937, the northern and southern blocks of Prome Court were converted into offices for the Public Works Department. The Secretariat (1), where the department was previously housed, had become overcrowded due to the reorganization of government administrative bodies following the separation of Myanmar from India.

In 1948, after Independence, Prome Court became the Deputy Prime Minister's Office and the Ministry of Foreign Affairs. Later, the entire complex was taken over by the Ministry.

PRESENT

This building has been mostly empty since the Ministry of Foreign Affairs moved the bulk of its offices to the new capital of Nay Pyi Taw in 2005; the Ministry's remaining offices are housed in a building located behind the former Prome Court.

The surrounding neighbourhood is part of the diplomatic quarter, with embassies and ambassadorial residences. As the building was once used for residential flats it would be most easily appropriated as a high-end apartment block or boutique hotel.

Maurice Collis and the book he researched in part while living at Prome Court

30 STATE FINE ARTS SCHOOL

formerly
CHIN TSONG PALACE

Location: Kaba Aya Pagoda Road

Built: 1915-1919

Architect/ Contractor: Clark & Greig (contractor)

This lavish mansion displays an idiosyncratic blend of European and Chinese architecture; the pagoda-like central tower is adorned with marble Grecian columns, while European-style archways are decorated with Chinese woodcarvings.

PAST

This five-storey home had a dining room that seated 100 guests and was an ostentatious display of extreme wealth. Set in rolling gardens that were immaculately landscaped with streams, ornamental bridges, and sculptures, it was designed as the ultimate pleasure palace of the shipping and rubber baron Lim Chin Tsong.

This building's construction was something of an event in Yangon at the time. A British woman who grew up in the city recalled that her family often drove past to see how it was progressing: "An enormous tiered Chinese-style temple was gradually taking shape with green tiled roofs and carved wood work, windows and doors. Around the enormous gardens, dozens of gardeners laboured fashioning mystical dragons and beasts from the trees."

Lim Chin Tsong was the son of a Chinese immigrant who set up a trading firm in Myanmar in the early 1860s. His father sent him to St. Paul's High School [3], where he became a star pupil. After his father's death, Lim Chin Tsong took over the family business and expanded it in all directions; he purchased a fleet of steamers that ferried passengers and freight between Yangon, southern China, and the Straits Settlements. He invested in a plantation, sugar refinery, mills, cotton, and groundnut oil production, and also surveyed for gold, copper, and tin. As a successful businessman he became a member of the Municipal Committee and was made an honorary magistrate. He also bred racehorses and sponsored what the *Rangoon Times* referred to as the "only polo tournament of any real consequence in Burma".

In the 1924 guide *Seaports of the Far East*, the interior of Lim Chin Tsong's mansion was described in glowing terms: "The magnificence of its equipment in rare and valuable furniture, in statuary, pictures, articles of gold, silver, ivory, curios of every description and in the richness and novelty of its electrical illumination, is in keeping with the beauty of the chromatic effects of walls and ceilings, the carving of the woodwork, the marble floors and staircases, the huge pillars gleaming with inlaid mother-of-pearl, and the greatness of the perspectives of halls, corridors and noble apartments, where the old and the new, the East and the West are expressed of a harmony that is remarkable and unique."

Various legends surround the fate of Lim Chin Tsong, who died in the 1920s. Some say he committed suicide by jumping from the tower; he reportedly went bankrupt after two of his steamers sank on the way to Amoy (now Xiamen), China. Another version has it that he was involved in counterfeiting money and had to flee the country when one of his many wives turned out to be investigating him; it is rumoured that a secret underground tunnel provides an exit route from the house to the nearby lake.

The British government later took over the building and occasionally held public viewings for selected groups of visitors.

During World War II, the Japanese army used the property as a radio station. On recapturing the city, Allied forces found the building in good condition, apart from some military vandalism on the walls. Earth ramparts were still in place, protecting the exterior from shrapnel, and the once-manicured lawns were riddled with foxholes, gun placements, and planted crops. An R-25 platform rifle was positioned in the tower, aimed at the palace gates and any potential intruders.

After Independence, the mansion was used as a hotel called the Kanbawza Palace. The first floor was well-suited for this purpose, as it had numerous spacious bedrooms with en suite bathrooms and dressing rooms.

Later, the mansion was repurposed as the Ministry of Culture with the Minister's office located at the top of the tower, affording him a spectacular 360-degree view over the city, which encompassed the Shwedagon pagoda and Inya Lake. The Ministry moved out after the government established the new capital at Nay Pyi Taw in 2005.

PRESENT

The compound is still owned by the Ministry of Culture and is currently being used as the State Fine Arts School. With only a few of the former bedrooms on the first floor currently in use as studios for art students, much of the mansion is now in need of repair.

POTENTIAL

This building is a truly unique example of a private residence that blends both Eastern and Western artistic and architectural influences in Yangon. It could serve as a splendid museum and venue for cultural events, and has already been used for art exhibitions.

In conservation terms, this building's most obvious parallel is the Cheong Fatt Tze Mansion in Penang, Malaysia. Built around the same time as this building, the Mansion was commissioned by a Chinese immigrant with a similar rags-to-riches story. In 1990 the by-then dilapidated mansion was sold to conservation-minded owners who undertook the job of restoring it to its original splendour. The renovation involved both local artisans and Cantonese carpenters brought in from China to repair the timber carvings, door and window frames, and balusters. The mansion is now a much sought after boutique hotel and a prominent stop on the Penang tourist trail, as well as being a venue for exhibitions, concerts, weddings, and other public activities.

Interiors of the Chin Tsong Palace

The Chin Tsong palace with protective earth walls and foxholes during World War II when it was used as a Japanese radio station, Glenn S. Hensley, 1945

THE STORY OF LIM CHIN TSONG'S MURALS

One day, while Lim Chin Tsong was visiting London, he had lunch at a Chinese restaurant in Piccadilly Circus. He asked the proprietor to recommend a good artist to come to Myanmar and paint the walls of his new mansion. The proprietor immediately introduced him to a young married couple seated nearby. The couple happened to be the artists Ernest and Dod Proctor (both of whom would later achieve enough fame to have their work hung in London's Tate Gallery and National Portrait Gallery). At the time, though, they were young and broke and easily wooed by the adventure of travelling to a faraway land.

The frescos the Proctors painted still exist on the first floor of the Chin Tsong Palace (picture opposite, bottom right), though they have been retouched since they were first painted. They are Chinese scenes, nicely executved but unremarkable, and contain no hint of the artistic talent the couple would exhibit in their later years.

"The Chin Tsong Palace building is the most interesting modern building I have been in in Yangon," says Andrew Ranard, author of *Burmese Painting*. *"Myanmar has its rich history in mural depiction, much of which has been destroyed or deteriorated. Though the Proctor's work here is not their best, it does count for something, and should be preserved."*

AFTERWORD

I was born after the socialist government took over the country. Soon afterwards, all foreign investment and private enterprise was curtailed. In my childhood I used to overhear my mother and aunts talking about the "good old times", as they referred to the pre-war colonial period. They often reminisced about luxury items imported from England, reliable municipal services, and the modes of transport available at that time (such as electric trams, horse-drawn dogcarts, and rickshaws).

Then, during World War II, people were forced to leave their possessions behind and flee for their lives. Many perished. The war scarred Yangon. Afterwards, the already enormous task of rebuilding the city was further challenged by instability in the countryside due to the civil war and this led to a great influx of rural migrants to the city. As a result, the post-war government had to extend the metropolitan boundaries by setting up three satellite towns to accommodate the growing population. While modern buildings replaced old ones or were constructed outside the original boundaries, many damaged buildings were repaired and reused. After 1962, when the socialist government created a closed-door political and economic system, most commercial buildings were turned into public offices. Since urbanization in the socialist era occurred at such a slow pace, the city's landscape, dense with colonial-era structures, remained little changed during that time even though the population of Yangon had multiplied five-fold since before World War II. Though they were hardly looked after, the grandeur of these thick-walled and brick-pointed buildings became a part of people's daily lives.

The school I attended for my primary and secondary education had been an early 20th-century Methodist girls' school that was tucked in between a Methodist church and a mysterious-looking missionary house; the school had been nationalised during the socialist period and turned into a public high school. Like me, many other Yangon residents attended colonial-style missionary schools in their childhood and later went on to hold office jobs or conduct businesses in and around the high-ceilinged colonial buildings of the city's central business district. Even the hospitals they were born in were built around the turn of the 20th century.

The architectural education we have been receiving since the programme was established in Myanmar in 1954 has been based on Western architectural theory and British construction techniques. Surviving colonial-era buildings exemplify how these architectural theories were practically applied in Myanmar. Irrespective of whether the colonial era is perceived as good or bad by the people who lived under it, there is no doubt that those times have left their mark to this day. We still use old British names when referring to certain streets or areas, such as Fraser, Hermitage, Windermere, Goodliffe, Halpin,

Monkey point, etc., despite the government's continuous efforts to rename them. Even within the context of nationalist resistance, this tangible and intangible colonial heritage is part of our lives. For over a hundred years the character of modern Yangon has been shaped by the dominating form of the Shwedagon Pagoda and other holy structures of different religions that make up the city's skyline, as well as by the colonial buildings modified for the local tropical climate, shady trees, wetted down roads, rivers, creeks, natural lakes, and parks.

Since the 1988 uprising and consequent decline of the socialist era, the city has undergone a more rapid pace of development, with a building boom and the extension of the city limits. The regulatory framework is far behind the speed of activities and falls short of ensuring that the city's growth is properly regulated for the wellbeing of its citizens. Conservation efforts on historical buildings and sites have been modest. Moreover, ministerial offices were relocated to Nay Pyi Taw in 2005 and the buildings left behind have been mostly uncared for, even after the additional damage caused by Cyclone Nargis in 2008. Recent bidding over former ministerial offices poses another threat to these buildings and the social networks they support. Therefore, it is now critical that conservation efforts are backed up by strong government action. This book contains 30 of the most stunning colonial-era buildings in downtown Yangon, beautifully profiled by the writer Sarah Rooney. They are included in the list of 189 heritage buildings compiled by the Yangon City Development Committee [YCDC] in 2001 based on their historical and architectural value. This book does not cover the many old religious buildings [Buddhist pagodas and monasteries, Hindu temples, churches, mosques, etc.] and other structures [missionary school buildings and markets] that are equally magnificent in their own right. Also excluded are some of the privately owned buildings, which should be prioritised given their role in the history of Yangon and the country as a whole. For instance, we could still save the residence of the first Myanmar architect, U Tha Tun, which he designed for himself in the 1930s. And these examples are in Yangon alone; the list of colonial heritage worth protecting should surely be extended beyond this one city to include Sittwe, Myeik, and Mawlamyaing, all of which have even older colonial-era structures as they came under British control before Yangon, in 1824.

By conveying the beauty and significance of these buildings, I sincerely hope that this book will motivate future efforts in conservation and urban redevelopment.

Moe Moe Lwin
General Secretary of the Association of Myanmar Architects

OLD STREET NAMES

After Myanmar gained Independence from Britain in 1948, many of the city's streets were officially renamed. Names chosen during British times often commemorated notable colonial personages. Though, as B. R. Pearn wryly notes in his book, *A History of Rangoon*, the process was not always done in a meritorious manner: "For the more important roads, it was scandalously said, Lord Dalhousie [Governor-General of India] was personally responsible and distributed the streets among the names of his favourites during the consumption of after-dinner port."

Street names mentioned in this book are listed here alphabetically, followed by their original names and historical notes.

Anawrahta Road – **Fraser Street**, after Lieutenant Alexander Fraser who drew up the plans for Yangon city. The far western end was called **Canal Street** and the far eastern stretch was called **Bigandet Street**, after Bishop Bigandet who founded St Paul's High School (3). The current street name commemorates the 11th century monarch, King Anawrahta, who founded the ancient kingdom of Bagan and is considered one of the three great unifiers of the Myanmar nation.

Bo Aung Kyaw Street – **Sparks Street**, after Captain T. P. Sparks, who became Deputy Commissioner of Yangon after the British conquest in 1852. Before taking on the job he translated Buddhist legends into English, most notably *The Decisions of Princess Thoo-Dharma Tsari* (Mawlamyaing, 1851). The current street name memorialises Aung Kyaw, a student killed by policemen during a protest against British rule in 1938.

Bogyoke Aung San Road – the western stretch was called **Commissioner's Road** as the residence of the first British Commissioner, Sir Arthur Phayre, was located there. Heading eastward, from the railway station onwards, the street was called **Montgomerie Street**, after Dr. William Montgomerie, one of the original city planners. Today, the street is named in honour of General Aung San, leader of Myanmar's Independence struggle and founding father of the army.

Lanmadaw Street – **Godwin Road**, after the British officer Sir Henry Thomas Godwin who fought in both the first and second Anglo-Burmese wars; during the latter he was commander of the invading British troops. He died in India in 1853, shortly after capturing Yangon.

Mahabandoola Garden – Fytche Square, after Sir Albert Fytche, who was Commissioner of Burma [1867-1871]. Fytche later published a book about the country called *Burma Past & Present* [1878] and left his legacy in the scientific names of two local species he identified; an orchid called *Dendrobium fytchianum* and the Mountain Bamboo Partridge [*Bambusicola fytchii*].

Mahabandoola Garden Street – Barr Street, after an Assistant Commissioner called G. E. Barr. In *A History of Rangoon*, Pearn alludes that this choice may have had more to do with the alleged drinking session than with considered decision making: "That Phayre [see entry below] should be so honoured is reasonable; but why juniors such as Barr?" he wrote. "The selection appears to have been highly arbitrary and thoughtless."

Mahabandoola Road – Dalhousie Street, after James Broun-Ramsay, or Lord Dalhousie, who served as the Governor-General of India [1848-1856]. Lord Dalhousie oversaw the second Anglo-Burmese war, which resulted in the capture of Yangon and annexation of lower Myanmar. The current name commemorates General Mahabandoola, who died in action during the first Anglo-Burmese War and is remembered for his brave resistance to British rule.

Pansodan Street – Phayre Street, after Sir Arthur Purves Phayre, first Commissioner of Burma [1862-1867]. Like his successor, Fytche, Phayre left a legacy of writings and discoveries; he wrote the first comprehensive English-language history of the country, *History of Burma* [1883], and discovered new animal species in Myanmar, two of which were named after him [Phayre's Leaf Monkey and Phayre's Squirrel].

Shwebontha Street – Mogul Street, after the Muslim merchants who lived and worked in this area.

Theinbyu Road – Judah Ezekiel Street, after a wealthy Jewish businessman and philanthropist who lived in Yangon in the 19th century. Ezekiel was known for his generosity and great girth; he reportedly fell through the floor of a *gharry* [a horse-drawn carriage] and was extracted only after some difficulty. In addition to his civic donations, Ezekiel paid for the metalling of this road and left 9 rupees a month in his will to keep it clean after his death.

SOURCES

Books

- *A Civil Servant in Burma*, Sir Herbert Thirkell White (E. Arnold, London, 1913)
- *A Handbook on Burma* (Directorate of Information, Rangoon, 1968)
- *A Handbook for Travellers in India, Burma and Ceylon* (John Murray, London, 1924 and 1955 editions)
- *A History of Modern Burma*, Michael W. Charney (Cambridge University Press, United Kingdom, 2009)
- *A History of Rangoon*, B. R. Pearn (Rangoon Municipal Corporation, Rangoon, 1939)
- *Almost Englishmen*, Ruth Fredman Cernea (Lexington Books, United Kingdom, 2007)
- *An Imperial Vision: Architecture and Britain's Raj*, Thomas R. Metcalf (University of California Press, 1989)
- *Baghdad to Bombay: In the Kitchens of my Cousins*, Pearl Sofaer (Paper Jam Publishing, United States, 2008)
- *Bombay Gothic*, Christopher W. London (India Book House, Mumbai, 2002)
- *Burma*, John L. Christian (Collins, London, 1945)
- *Burma*, R. Talbot Kelly (Albert and Charles Black, London, 1909)
- *Burma: A Travel Survival Kit*, Tony Wheeler (Lonely Planet, USA/Australia, 1979)
- *Burmah: A Photographic Journey 1855-1925*, Noel F. Singer (Kiscadale, United Kingdom, 1993)
- *Burma During the Japanese Occupation, Vol. 1* (Burma Intelligence Bureau, India, 1943)
- *Burma Independence Celebrations* (Department of Information and Broadcasting, Government of the Union of Burma, Rangoon, 1948)
- *Burmese Painting: A Linear and Lateral History*, Andrew Ranard (Silkworm Books, Thailand, 2009)
- *Canoe to Mandalay*, R. Raven-Hart (Frederick Muller, London, 1939)
- *Fiery Dragons: Banks, Moneylenders and Microfinance in Burma*, Sean Turnell (Silkworm Books, Thailand, 2009)
- *From Sea to Sea and Other Sketches: Letters of Travel*, Rudyard Kipling (United Kingdom, 1890)
- *Grindlays 1828-1978*, Lord Aldington (GB, London, 1978)
- *History of the Burmah Oil Company, Vol II, 1924-1966* (William Heinemann, London, 1988)
- *I Lived in Burma*, E. C. V. Foucar (Dobson Books, London, 1956)
- *Irrawaddy Flotilla*, Alistair McCrae (James Paton, United Kingdom, 1978)
- *Journey Through Burma in 1936*, Prince Damrong Rajanubhab (River Books, Thailand, 1999)
- *Lines from a Shining Land*, Derek Brooke-Wavell, ed. (Britain-Burma Society, United Kingdom, 1998)
- *Mall's Directory* (Unique Publishing House, Rangoon, 1941)
- *My Burma*, U Ba U (Taplinger Publishing Company, New York, 1959)
- *Old Rangoon*, Noel F. Singer (Kiscadale Publications, Scotland, 1995)
- *Rangoon: A Pocket Guide* (Ministry of Information, Rangoon, 1954)
- *Rangoon: Sights and Institutions* (Ministry of Culture, Rangoon, 195-?)
- *Realms of Silver*, Sir Compton MacKenzie (Routledge & Kegan Paul, London, 1954)
- *Seaports of the Far East*, Allister MacMillan (Collingridge, London, 1924)
- *Scenes in Burma: An Album of 125 Views* (Whiteaway, Laidlaw & Co., Rangoon, 190-?)

- *Splendours of the Raj*, Philip Davies (John Murray, London, 1985)
- *Stones of Empire: The Buildings of British India*, Jan Morris (Penguin, United Kingdom, 1983)
- *The Burma Yearbook 1957-58* (Ministry of Information, Rangoon, 1958)
- *The Extraordinary Museums of Southeast Asia*, Kristin Kelly (Harry N. Abrams, New York, 2001)
- *The Magic Guide to Burma*, Roy Hudson (Hudson's Pamphlet Series, 1977)
- *The Moon Princess: Memories of the Shan States*, Sao Sanda (River Books, Thailand, 2008)
- *The Strand Yangon*, Andreas Augustin (The Most Famous Hotels in the World, United Kingdom, 2003)
- *Trials in Burma*, Maurice Collis (Faber & Faber, London, 1938)
- *Twentieth Century Impressions of Burma*, Arnold Wright, ed. (Lloyd's Greater Britain Publishing Company, United Kingdom, 1910)
- *Who's Who in Burma* (Indo-Burma Publishing Agency, Calcutta & Rangoon, 1927)
- *Yangon: Old and New Pictures of the Garden City*, U Ye Thu and Edwin Briels (Yone Kyi Chet Book House, Yangon, 2004)
- *Yangon: The Garden City* (Yangon City Development Committee, Yangon, 1995)
- *Yangon Yazawin Thamaing*, U Thein Maung (Thadin Sasaya, Yangon, 2011)

Others

- "Architecture in India", by John Begg, Consulting Architect to the Government of India (lecture read before the Royal Institute of British Architects, RIBA, 12 April 1920, and published in *Journal of the Royal Institute of British Architects*, 8 May 1920)
- 'Asia Urbanites and Cosmopolitan Cultures in Bangkok, Penang and Rangoon, 1910-1940', by Su Lin Lewis (PhD Dissertation, Cambridge University, 2010)
- "European Architecture in India", by James Ransome, Consulting Architect to the Government of India (lecture read before the Royal Institute of British Architects, RIBA, 23 January 1905, and published in *Journal of the Royal Institute of British Architects*, 1905)
- *Historical Walks in Yangon*, map by Myanmar Heritage Trust (Silkworm Books, Thailand, 2009)
- Royal Institute of British Architects, RIBA, nomination papers (available at the RIBA library, London)
- *The Rangoon Times*, Christmas Editions (1912-1925)
- *India Office Records (British Library, London):*
  - Administration Report of the Commissioners for the Port of Rangoon (1925-1928)
  - Administration Report of the Public Works Department, Burma, Buildings and Roads Branch, (1880-1940)
  - Annual Report on Architectural Work in India (1907-1923)
  - Government of India Building Designs (pamphlet by James Ransome, FRIBA, 1909)
  - Report on the Working of the Rangoon Municipality (1908-1940)

ACKNOWLEDGEMENTS

With thanks the following individuals and institutions (in alphabetical order):

Vicky Bowman, Daw Chaw Kalyar, Gerry Fox, Patricia Herbert, Zunetta Herbert, Junior Win, Dr. Kyaw Lat, U Myo Min, Charlotte O'Sullivan, Andrew Ranard, John Randall, Dawn Rooney, U Soe Win, U Sun Oo, Robert Taylor, Dr. Thant Myint-U, Dr. Thant Thaw Kaung, U Thaw Kaung, Daw Thynn Thynn Aye, U Win Myint, and U Zaw Lynn.

The Burmah Oil Company records (BP Archive, University of Warwick), the India Office Records at the British Library, Lloyds Banking Group Archives and Museums, the archives and library of the Royal Institute of British Architects, the Standard Chartered Bank Archives (housed at the London Metropolitan Archives), the Irrawaddy Flotilla Company records (Maritime Archives of the National Museums, Liverpool).

Note: While some buildings profiled in this book feature a section entitled "Potential", those that do not are currently occupied and have yet to announce any change of ownership.

PHOTOGRAPHIC CREDITS

COVER
Natthaphat Meksriwan

INTRODUCTION
Page 6, 10 · Natthaphat Meksriwan

SECTION A
Page 20-21 · Whiteaway, Laidlaw & Co. Album, c. 190-?, courtesy Patricia Herbert

Building 1
Page 22 · Natthaphat Meksriwan
Page 25 · Courtesy Nic Dunlop/Panos
Page 26 · Who's Who in Burma, 1927
Page 27 · Whiteaway, Laidlaw & Co., Album, c. 190-?, courtesy Patricia Herbert

Building 2
Page 28, 30 · Natthaphat Meksriwan
Page 31 · Courtesy the Royal Incorporation of Architects in Scotland

Building 3
Page 32, 34 · Natthaphat Meksriwan
Page 35 · Image of Pablo Neruda, photographer unknown
Page 36 · Sarah Rooney

SECTION B
Page 38-39 · Natthaphat Meksriwan

Building 4
Page 40, 41 · Natthaphat Meksriwan
Page 43 (above) · Natthaphat Meksriwan
Page 43 (below) · Glenn S. Hensley, 1945, from Digital South Asia Library, University of Chicago

Building 5
Page 44, 45, 46 · Natthaphat Meksriwan
Page 45 · (above) Courtesy Sarah Rooney
Page 47 · Reproduced with permission from the artist, MKM

Building 6
Page 48 · Daw Thynn Thynn Aye
Page 50 · Sarah Rooney
Page 51 · Photograph of Khin Myo Chit, courtesy Khin Myo Chit Family, Yangon; others, Burmese-language magazines

Building 7
Page 52, 53 · Natthaphat Meksriwan

Building 8
Pages 54-56 · Natthaphat Meksriwan
Page 57 · Whiteaway, Laidlaw & Co., Album, c. 190-?, courtesy Patricia Herbert

SECTION C
Page 62-63 · Natthaphat Meksriwan

Building 9
Page 65 · Natthaphat Meksriwan
Page 66 · (left) Frank Bond, 1945, (right) Glenn S. Hensley, 1945, both from Digital South Asia Library, University of Chicago

Building 10
Pages 67, 69 · Natthaphat Meksriwan
Page 70 · Rangoon: Sights and Institutions, 1954

Building 11
Pages 71-72 · Natthaphat Meksriwan
Page 73 · Courtesy private collection

SECTION D
Pages 76-77 · Natthaphat Meksriwan

Building 12
Pages 78, 80 · Natthaphat Meksriwan

Building 13
Pages 81-82 · Natthaphat Meksriwan
Page 84 · Collection of Paw Oo Thet Family, Mandalay. Courtesy Silkworm Books

Building 14
Pages 86-87 · Natthaphat Meksriwan
Pages 88-89 · Courtesy Irrawaddy Flotilla Company Collection, National Museums Liverpool

Building 15
Pages 90-91 · Natthaphat Meksriwan
Page 93 · Felice Beato, c. 1890

Building 16
Page 92 · Natthaphat Meksriwan
Page 94 · Courtesy Lloyds Banking Group Archives and Museums

Building 17
Pages 95-96 · Natthaphat Meksriwan
Pages 96 and 98 · Plans reproduced with permission from Standard Chartered Bank

Essay: Constructing Yangon's Colonial Core
Page 99 · Natthaphat Meksriwan

SECTION E
Pages 104-105 · Natthaphat Meksriwan

Building 18
Pages 106-108 · Natthaphat Meksriwan

Building 19
Pages 109, 110 · [above] Natthaphat Meksriwan
Page 109 · [below] Charlotte O'Sullivan

Building 20
Page 110 Natthaphat Meksriwan
Pages 111-112 [above] · Natthaphat Meksriwan
Page 112 [below] · Courtesy John Randall Books of Asia

Building 21
Pages 115-116 · Natthaphat Meksriwan

Building 22
Pages 118-120 · Natthaphat Meksriwan

Building 23
Pages 121, 123 [above] · Natthaphat Meksriwan
Page 123 [below] · Reproduced with permission from the Royal Commission on the Ancient and Historical Monuments of Scotland

Building 24
Pages 124-125 · Natthaphat Meksriwan
Page 125 [top right and bottom] · Reproduced with permission from the British Steel Collection

Building 25
Pages 126-127 · Natthaphat Meksriwan
Page 127 [bottom left] · Frank Bond, 1945, from Digital South Asia Library, University of Chicago
Page 127 [bottom right] · Charlotte O'Sullivan

Essay: Yangon Renovations
Pages 128-129 · Courtesy 50th Street Bar & Grill
Page 130 · Courtesy Monsoon Restaurant & Bar
Page 131 · Courtesy Gallery 65
Pages 132-133 · Courtesy SPINE Architects

SECTION F
Pages 134-135 · Natthaphat Meksriwan

Building 26
Pages 136-137 · Natthaphat Meksriwan

Building 27
Pages 139-141 · Natthaphat Meksriwan

Building 28
Page 142 · Yanni Kronenberg
Page 143 · Postcard, D. A. Ahuja

Building 29
Pages 144-145 · Yanni Kronenberg
Page 145 · Image of Rudyard Kipling, photographer unknown
Page 146 · Yanni Kronenberg
Page 147 · Image of Maurice Collis, photographer unknown, jacket of Penguin Books; [right] Yanni Kronenberg

Building 30
Page 148 · Charlotte O'Sullivan
Page 150 · Sarah Rooney, [top right corner] Charlotte O'Sullivan
Page 151 · Glenn S. Hensley, 1945, from Digital South Asia Library, University of Chicago

Maps
Page 16-19 · Natthaphat Meksriwan
Page 102-103 · Tourist's Map of Rangoon, Burma Survey Dept. [M.P.O.] Rangoon, undated

INDEX